A Drop in the Bucket

A Drop in the Bucket

The Joys, Sorrows, and Horrors of Medical Missions

Dolores Edwards

iUniverse, Inc.
New York Lincoln Shanghai

A Drop in the Bucket

The Joys, Sorrows, and Horrors of Medical Missions

Copyright © 2007 by Dolores Edwards

All rights reserved. No part of this book may be used or reproduced by any means, graphic, electronic, or mechanical, including photocopying, recording, taping or by any information storage retrieval system without the written permission of the publisher except in the case of brief quotations embodied in critical articles and reviews.

iUniverse books may be ordered through booksellers or by contacting:

iUniverse
2021 Pine Lake Road, Suite 100
Lincoln, NE 68512
www.iuniverse.com
1-800-Authors (1-800-288-4677)

ISBN-13: 978-0-595-41599-1 (pbk)
ISBN-13: 978-0-595-85947-4 (ebk)
ISBN-10: 0-595-41599-7 (pbk)
ISBN-10: 0-595-85947-X (ebk)

Printed in the United States of America

The views expressed in this work are solely those of the author and do not necessarily reflect the views of the publisher, and the publisher hereby disclaims any responsibility for them.

"We are simply God's servants, by whom you were led to believe. Each one of us does the work the Lord gave him to do."
"God will reward each one according to the work he has done."
"For we are partners working together for God, and you are God's field. You are also God's building."
"Using the gift that God gave me, I did the work of an expert builder and laid the foundation, and another man is building on it. But each one must be careful how he builds."

1 Corinthians 3: 5,8,9,10
Today's English Version

Isaiah 40:15 . . . "Surely the nations are like a drop in a bucket" . . . .

Unless otherwise indicated, Bible quotations are taken from Life Application Study Bible, New International Version of the Bible. Copyright 1991 by Tyndale House Publishers, Inc.

Contents

List of Illustrations ix

Acknowledgments xi

Preface xiii

Prologue xv

Chapter 1: Paso a Paso se Va Lejos 1
(The road to Rome (Colombia) begins but with a single step)

Chapter 2: A Buena Hambre, No Hay Mal Pan 29
(If you're hungry, any food will taste good)

Chapter 3: Querer es Poder 45
(Where there is a will there is a way)

Chapter 4: A Grandes Males, Grandes Remedios 90
(Great needs require great solutions)

Chapter 5: La Necesidad Abre la Puerta de Muchos Logros 97
(Necessity is the mother of invention)

Chapter 6: Para no Consarle con el Cuento 120
(To make a long story short)

Chapter 7: Cerrando con Broche de Oro 140
(Finishing well)

APPENDIX 145

GLOSSARY OF SPANISH WORDS AND PHRASES 149

List of Illustrations

Map of South America ii
Map of Colombia with mobile clinic sites xiv
Embera Indian mothers 36
Floating outhouse 85
Daniel—ex-street gang member 109
Refugee dwelling 126
Rural ambulance 128

Acknowledgments

Thanks to all the people who have encouraged me to put our experiences in book form, Vicky Brasington was the first. She has gone to be with the Lord, but her memory and encouragement lingers on. To my family for supporting me and putting up with my hectic schedule, it has been a long journey, but haven't we had a great time. To my daughter Barbara, who helped with the editing and especially to my daughter Jennifer, who spent hours helping to revise and edit, my heartfelt thanks to each of them. To my daughter-in-law, Dunia, who helped with the Spanish chapter titles. To my husband, Robert, who is a vital part of the book. My thanks to all our Colombian brethren and missionary colleagues with whom we have worked over the years. Thanks to Charles Fake who helped scan my pictures. Most important, is my thanks to my Lord, who allowed us to be a part of His great work in Colombia for thirty years.

Grateful appreciation is extended to the following for permission to quote from their copyrighted materials:

VOICES OF THE FAITHFUL by Beth Moore compiled by Kim P. Davis, Published by Integrity Publishers, Copyright 2005 International Mission Board of the Southern Baptist Convention and Elizabeth Moore.

Preface

Barbara Bush in her memoir wrote that she *"used a very selective memory of [her] early years and it was the truth as [she] saw it."* Like her I tried to tell the truth as I saw it. Several people were interviewed in my research. Our shared adventures were perceived from different viewpoints. I wrote this book using vignettes encompassing our thirty years on the mission field. It is in chronological order, more or less, incorporating interviews, excerpts from letters that I had written to family and friends over the years, and my own interpretations.

There is such a great need in Colombia and we could not fill every need. What we accomplished was just a drop in the bucket. We had to remember that drops fill the bucket, and each need that we met helped to fill that bucket. God worked through us to help many people; it was such a joy seeing His handiwork.

I hope that you can laugh with us, and cry with us, as you read about the frustrations and joys that we experienced during our thirty years on the field of medical missions.

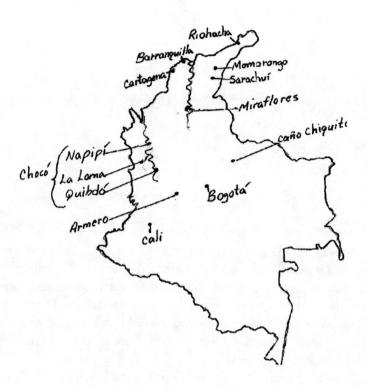

Prologue

There were several "*moscas*"* asking questions about us. Our hosts didn't trust one of the "*moscas*" who was known to have harbored guerrillas the month before. They began to spread the word that we were to leave at 5:00 AM on Thursday morning. At 3:00 AM Wednesday, our guide silently poled our dugout canoe downstream to safety. Early Thursday morning the guerrillas arrived at the village looking for us.

(*Mosca*s is the word used by the local people to designate informants for the Marxist guerrillas groups.)

Chapter 1

Paso a Paso se Va Lejos
(The road to Rome (Colombia) begins but with a single step)

In 1972 Robert was in private practice in Lake Jackson, Texas. We had just purchased our "dream home," had our fourth child, and were happy living close to both of our families. As members of First Baptist Church in Lake Jackson we were actively involved in several ministries such as outreach, singing in the choir, women's missionary union (WMU), teaching Sunday school and Training Union. The church was very mission minded and several members often went on volunteer mission trips. Dr. W. D. Nickelson, or Dr. Nick as everyone affectionately called him, had just returned from a mission trip to Yemen. While he was sharing his experiences in Yemen and the great needs there, Robert felt that God was calling him into full time mission work. When he came home and shared this with me, my first response was, "Your out of your cotton picking mind!" I struggled several weeks; I informed God just why I was not qualified to be a missionary. Our eleven-year-old son, Mike, came to us one day and said, "Mom and Dad, have ya'll ever thought about being medical missionaries?" As my jaw dropped, I looked upward and thought, "OK Lord if that is really what you want us to do." We contacted the Foreign Mission Board (FMB) of the Southern Baptist Convention (SBC) in June 1972 and I expected the door to close at any time. Part of the appointment process for missionaries is to write an autobiography.

This autobiography showed me that the Lord had been preparing us for mission work all our lives. We were appointed to Colombia, South America in October 1972. After our appointment, we received a call from Colombia saying that they had been praying for a surgeon for ten years. This helped confirm our decision.

Dr. Nick promised to pray for us every day and we know that he did until the day he died.

We packed everything and left in January 1973 to attend Southwestern Baptist Theological Seminary in Fort Worth. After one semester there we went to Pine Mountain, Georgia for fourteen weeks of missionary orientation. A small two-bedroom vacation cottage was provided for our four children and us. Mike, twelve years old; Barbara, eleven years old; Charles, nine years old; and Jennifer, two years old shared one tiny bedroom with bunk beds. The six of us shared one small bathroom. It was a great transition time for us but also a stressful time. We made a game of it and everyone enjoyed the time but was ready to leave.

*   *   *   *

In December 1973 we traveled to San Jose, Costa Rica where we spent a year in language school. It was an extraordinary year in which we began learning not only the Spanish language but also the culture. The people of Costa Rica are delightful and they love to help you.

My parents came to visit us for a week. We traveled by public bus since we did not have a car. One day as we were standing in a crowded bus, my Dad cried out, "Someone took my wallet!" I tossed three-year-old Jennifer into the arms of my mother, and Dad and I took off running after the two thieves. We caught them and the police were soon there to help us. One guy was begging and pleading with us professing his innocence. All that I could think to say in my limited Spanish was, "Phooey! *Usted es cupable* (you are guilty). After frisking them and not finding Dad's wallet, the policemen said that they probably had an accomplice who ran off with the stolen goods and was waiting to divide up the loot with them later. One of the policemen took us aside and asked us what was in the wallet. Dad told him, "Credit cards, drivers license, and about $50." The policeman then returned to the thieves, and speaking to the other policeman, told him that there had been credit cards, a driver's license, and about $250. They had to release the thieves for lack of evidence, but they winked at us and told us that there would be trouble that night when these two thieves joined their accomplice and asked for their share of the $250 loot. Meanwhile, Jennifer was thoroughly enjoying the events, but Mother was not too happy. Nevertheless, seeing two gringos running and screaming down the street and tackling two thieves had entertained local people.

* * * *

An excerpt from a letter written by Robert to his Dad in October 1974: ... "I spent two weeks in Honduras working with refugees from Hurricane Fifi. Before the flood they weren't too well off and now they really have a miserable outlook. The last weekend we were there another flood isolated us in El Progreso for two days. We set up a clinic in that city and from there went by helicopter to small isolated villages to vaccinate and treat mostly kids with diarrhea and upper respiratory infections as well as anemia and parasites. For the most part they probably have better medical care now than they have ever had. The problems will come much later when they don't have any harvest"

* * * *

While Robert was in Honduras, we had a minor emergency at home in San José. Jennifer (age 3) inserted a small metal disk from a necklace into her ear. Panicked, she started screaming and Carmen, our maid, hysterically wailed that Jennifer was going to die. I couldn't calm either one of them enough to find the object and remove it, so I took Jennifer to a clinic by taxi. I made the mistake of telling the driver why Jennifer was hysterical. I tried to explain that it was not an emergency, but he raced through the streets, not even stopping for stop signs. The inevitable happened. A motorcycle ran into us about four blocks from the clinic. Jennifer and I had to walk the rest of the way to the clinic. The "emergency" was seen two hours later by the doctor, and then, he could not find the object. The doctor and I laughed at our adventure and spent a few minutes talking about Honduras. He had worked with Robert for a few days during the hurricane disaster relief efforts.

* * * *

Corruption is rampant throughout Colombia. The mission had imported two vans from the States and was having difficulty getting them out of customs. The agent helping us do all the paper work reported that he had to grease the palms of a customs inspector "to improve his eyesight" because he couldn't see the serial number on the engine clearly enough to verify that it matched the import number. It is amazing to see how quickly his eyesight improved. When our household shipment arrived we had to have several pairs of eyes to prevent items from "accidently" slipping out of the crates and into someone's pocket or truck. We were fortunate that they did not remove everything from the crates to minutely examine each item as they sometimes did. The customs inspector had a mother who needed an operation, and Robert was able to make an appointment for her at our Baptist Clinic and for our other missionary doctor, George Kollmar, to do the surgery, if needed, at a reduced price. We discovered early that it pays to have contacts. It is called *palanca** or to have influence.

A few days after we arrived in Barranquilla we were invited to a Christmas drama at Belen Church. The church was packed, but they made room on a hard wooden bench for the six of us. And then the drama began. It lasted four long hours. There was no air conditioning, and it was a hot tropical afternoon in a room packed with hot bodies. I was so proud of the children, ages thirteen, twelve, ten, and three. Even though they were uncomfortable and couldn't understand much of what was happening, they behaved very well. Robert and I didn't understand everything either, but we all sat through the entire drama and afterwards, smiled and visited with the people. Two days later, the clinic gave us a welcoming party in the parking lot at the clinic. There were many people who recited poetry; others sang special music. There were welcoming speeches, and—*then*—Belen church presented their four hour drama again. The children all looked at me with dismay and said, "M—O—M!" I let them go into the clinic garden to play while Robert and I sat through the drama for a second time.

When I first saw the Baptist Clinic in Barranquilla, it reminded me of the old John Sealy Hospital in Galveston, Texas where I had trained back in the late '50's. It was about twenty-five years behind our stateside hospitals. They had the old metal patients' beds that had to be cranked to adjust. There was nothing disposable; everything was re-sterilized and recycled. There was no central air conditioning. A few of the private patients rooms had A/C window units. The people were not accustomed to air conditioning so they would leave the doors and windows open defeating the effect of the air conditioner. The kitchen area was open to the elements, and there were flies everywhere. Robert tried for years to get maintenance to put screens on the kitchen windows. He finally succeeded. The screens went up, but the flies were then all trapped inside. He said that he couldn't win.

* * * *

A story that I wrote that appeared on page 411 in *Voices of the Faithful* by Beth Moore (Published by Integrity Publishers 2005) … "When we first arrived in Colombia just before Christmas, one of our colleagues wanted our children to have a holiday to remember. At the time there were no frozen turkeys in the store, so Rosemary bought a live one and had it prepared for the meal. On Christmas Day, however, Rosemary discovered that her new helper had cut this turkey up for frying. The traditional turkey meal was ruined.

Two clever heads got together, and this problem was solved. My husband, Robert, was a surgeon, as was another missionary, so they proceeded to suture that turkey back to its original form! We baked our "very special turkey" as planned. It has been thirty years since that memorable event, and my children have never forgotten that first Christmas in Colombia.

This is a funny incident in the beginning of our missionary career, but it holds a spiritual truth that helped us through many discouraging and difficult times. A sense of humor, creativity and dependence on Him, especially when things did not turn out the way we planned, helped things work out for good. Sometimes we missed our family, comfortable lifestyle and friends in the States, but when we were in America, it didn't take us long to miss Colombia, the place God called us to minister.

As we are where God wants us to be, doing what He wants us to do, we can be happy knowing that we are in His will. He enjoys giving gifts to His children, even a very special turkey with a great story to remember forever" …

* * * *

We had been in town only two months when we experienced our first Barranquilla Carnival. The main parade called *La Batalla de Flores** was to begin a couple of blocks from where we were staying. I thought it would be fun to experience some of the culture of our adopted country. Robert had gone to a retreat outside of town with our two older children. I took our two youngest children, Charles and Jennifer and three other missionary kids about their same age to watch the parade. At first, it was exciting seeing all the floats being lined up and the beauty queens preparing to travel down the street. I noticed one of the beauty queens screaming and gesturing at some of the people around her. She was using words that were not in my vocabulary, but her meaning was very clear. Someone in the crowd asked to take her picture and suddenly she transformed into the sweet, smiling, demure beauty that she was supposed to be portraying. The crowd began to swell, and the alcoholic fumes from the breaths of people around us became stronger. There was pushing and shoving, and I started to panic. I had five small children with me, and I was afraid that we would get separated or that they would be crushed. A gentleman behind me noticed my distress and asked if he could help. He carried Jennifer on his shoulders and held the hands of two other children while I took the remaining two children. He elbowed and pushed a way through that drunken crowd to fresh air. When we were clear, he put Jennifer down, grinned, and asked if this was our first Carnival. Overwhelmed, I said, "Yes, and the last."

* * * *

The poverty in Colombia was staggering. We had not been there very long before a new *barrio** appeared overnight on public land that was created by spoil, dredged from the river. It consisted of 10,000 desperate people, who made their "home" out of whatever they could scrounge: cardboard cartons, tar paper, palm leaves, plastic garbage sacks, flattened tin cans, etc. There was no water to drink, no place to cook except on open fires, and no toilets. There was nothing but plenty of heat, humidity, and mosquitos, and this was better than what they had before. They named it *La Esperanza** or Hope.

* * * *

Living in Colombia, even in the cities, is a continual test of the upper limits of our physical, emotional and spiritual health. First, there is the simple matter of survival. You have to filter, then boil all drinking water. Telephones do not work the majority of the time, even buying groceries is a challenge. Nevertheless over the years it has improved.

When I go to the grocery store in the States, I am dumbfounded and go wild with all the availability and organization. Just going down the cereal aisle is confusing. When we first arrived in Colombia, the only cereal available was Corn Flakes and Rice Krispis, and they were usually stale. In the States, it is a major decision to decide between Plain Cheerios, Cheerios with Cinnamon, Honey nut Cheerios, Bran Cheerios, etc. The over abundance and availability of the same product with small variations is mind-boggling.

Rainy season last from May through November. There are two different kinds of rain. There is a nice, gentle rain and then there is a torrential downpour called an *aguacero*.* Barranquilla has no underground storm sewer system. With the sloping topography of the city, certain streets are designed to carry the water to designated streets that then carry it to the river. These designated streets in an instant become raging torrents that can sweep even big buses down the street to the river. These streets are called *arroyos**. Some who do not understand this phenomena try to cross these streets, and there is loss of life every year. There are dramatic rescues every rainy season.

* * * *

An excerpt from letter to Phoebe (my sister) March 1975: ... I hired a new maid yesterday, I hope I'm not sorry. She looks like a baby. She is only sixteen and fresh from the country. I spent all day showing her how to do things. We have to soak all our fruits and vegetables in a bleach solution to kill the amoebas. She wanted to know why we needed two sheets for each bed? When we showed her her own room to her, she cried. Magaly wanted to sleep with Jennifer, (age 3) because she had never slept by herself in her life. She always had several brothers or sisters sleeping in the same bed. (*She worked for us for the first four years that we were in Colombia, but we found her a job as a nanny when we left for a year-long furlough in the states. She was good with the children, but not much help in the house.*)

We went fishing with George Kollmar last week and it was a fascinating trip. We caught lots of fish but the trip alone would have been worth it. We saw five different types of parrots flying right over us and monkeys swinging in the trees along the bank. I heard a roar that sounded like a lion or tiger, and the fellows all laughed at me and strung me along for a while. It was a group of howler monkeys.

Along the bank of the river and in the middle of the bay were fisherman huts built on stilts. It amazed me that all had thatched roofs but many did not have walls, therefore no privacy. There were no solid floors, only planks set about three to four feet above the water. Babies were crawling on these planks, and I don't now how they didn't fall into the water and drown; unfortunately, some do. Little children, stark naked, about the age of Jennifer played in dugout canoes, poling them around their huts.

I got my driver's license today. Now I can get out with all the other maniacs on the street. The folks (our parents) probably told you how the Latins drive in

Costa Rica; well here, they don't drive quite as fast, but you never know what to expect. They may stop right in front of you without warning to buy cigarettes from a sidewalk vender or just to talk to someone. At night they often drive without putting on their lights "to conserve their battery". Jennifer has learned what to do in traffic. She was sitting in the front passenger seat (we had no air conditioning so the windows were open). I needed to turn right, but couldn't get into the right lane to do so. Jennifer put her little arm out the window and waved it up and down, and that lane of traffic came to a screeching halt and let me in so that I could turn. You have to learn the rules of driving etiquette here. The laws are the same as in the States, but very few know or obey them. For the whole city of Barranquilla, population more than a million, there is only one motorcycle traffic cop, so there is no enforcement of the laws.

Anyone who is an old car buff would have a ball here. Most of the cars are of the 1940 and 1950 vintage, and some are even older. We see lots with rumble seats. They are all in very good condition, painted and running smoothly. They are not luxury cars, but are working cars....

* * * *

An excerpt from letter to parents April 1975 ... Most of the places have fans but very few have air conditioning. Right now the wind blows you to pieces. The rainy season starts in May and last through November. They say that when it rains people stay at home because the streets literally become rivers. It is not a gentle rainfall but a torrent, fortunately, it doesn't rain everyday, and then only in the afternoons. It hasn't rained since we arrived, and it is really dry now. When we got here in December, we could clearly see the Sierra Nevada mountain range in Santa Marta, and in particular, the highest mountain peak in Colombia, "Cristóbal Colón," which is about sixty miles from here and has snow on it year round. In December we could clearly see the snow shining on top, but we can't even see the outline of the mountains now because it is so hazy from the dry heat haze and dust.

We will be so happy to leave this apartment. Right now I am listening to a North American mother scream and curse at her children, and to a Spanish family screaming at one another. One family has their record player going at top volume with Spanish music, and another North American family trying to drown out the Spanish music with American rock. Since we have to leave the doors and windows open, we get the full effect. Only two and a half months more of this, then we move into our house. Hallelujah!....

* * * *

Excerpts from personal report Robert wrote in August 1975: … My family and I have been enjoying Colombia for nine months now. As yet, I don't have my license to practice medicine here. (There is usually about this much delay). The Lord has given me work to do in administration, some in teaching, and in planning for the future of the Baptist Clinic. Above all He has given me the patience I need. I also have a better idea of the work I will be doing when I do get to practice.

I have had the opportunity of working with my pastor and his church in a mission in a small fishing village about thirty-five miles from Barranquilla. We load up our van with people and a portable pump organ each Thursday afternoon for services there. The village sits on a narrow strip of land separating a large salt water lake from the Caribbean sea. The population is about 3,000, the majority of which are children. The people fish from long, graceful dugout canoes with nets and hand lines. After several months of slow response, three teenage girls accepted Christ in March. We began having special Bible study for them, as well as the regular services and a special service for the little children. One day, I was teaching the three girls about the power of God's Word and said that there was no reason why next week we couldn't have ten more in this special study for believers. At that same time, in the regular service, nine people were making their profession of faith in Jesus Christ.

We have been overjoyed at the openness of the people in this fishing village. They listen, they read the material given out, and they are able to see the lives of the new Christians.

That is the sort of thing that happens on my "afternoon off" here in Colombia.…

* * * *

An excerpt from letter to my parents in 1975: … The whole city was without water for three days. We had been warned, so we had water stored in every container, shower stall, garbage can, and whatever else that could hold water. We also had two twenty-gallon jugs of bottled water, so we didn't hurt too much with this problem; but five minutes after the water came back on, the electricity went off for twelve hours. They fixed that, and it went off again. This went on four times, so that we were without electricity for a total of twenty hours. Everything in the freezer thawed out but thank goodness, we had not been living here long enough to have much in the freezer. This was Saturday. Sunday night the lights went off again, but only for three hours. Fortunately, I cook with propane gas. Tonight, I'm writing by candlelight because the lights have been off for four hours. I guess we have to be satisfied with water or electricity, not both at the same time. We run around turning everything off when the electricity goes off because often when it comes back on, it comes on with a big surge, and we have had light bulbs that have exploded and a small electric clock that has melted ...

※   ※   ※   ※

In 1975, Dr. Kenneth Taylor, one of the interpreters of the Living Bible, who was a classmate of George Kollmar at Wheaton College, spoke to all of the evangelical missionaries in our home. There were a total of fifty-two missionaries from all the different missionary groups.

That same year, I hosted the English Bible Club every Monday afternoon for children ages four to twelve. It was a combined effort of the South American Mission group, Brethren Missions, and our Southern Baptist group. We studied C. S. Lewis's *The Chronicles of Narnia*, had music time, did crafts and told Bible stories. There were twenty-two to twenty-five children attending. Robert and I also led the English-speaking Teen Club every Friday night. Working with us in teen club were Jeni Hester and several journeymen (short term missionaries). With this group we studied Bible scriptures, discussed teenage issues, sang, played games, and of course, ate lots of food. The first year, 1975, began slowly with only eight or nine attending each week. We ended that year with an average of forty teens attending.

※   ※   ※   ※

Trying to pack and decide what to take and what to leave the first time that we went to Colombia was very difficult. Many people gave us advice, but we later realized that each person's needs was different. We were told to pack things that would make us feel comfortable and at home. These included furniture, appliances, clothing, and toys for the children. We did not know what our living conditions would be, but we were told that there was a Sears department store in Barranquilla, so I made sure that all my appliances were Sears products. That was fine until the first time I needed repairs; I was told that my appliances were imported, so I had to personally order the parts from the States and then hope that they could do the repairs. Four years after we got there, Sears went out of business and left Barranquilla.

I brought a top of the line Singer Sewing Machine thinking that I would have to make the girls clothing, which I did for several years. After a couple of years, it needed some minor adjustments, and I took it into the Singer distributor store. The next morning, I went to pick it up, but they had been robbed during the night and my machine was one of those stolen. They were very sympathetic and said that they would compensate me. The first question that they asked was, "Did it have a motor?" I knew then that I was in trouble. They did replace it, but with a very inferior model. I later gave it to a lady in great need, and I found a dressmaker to make our clothing.

* * * *

An excerpt from letter to my parents December 1975: … We took eighteen of the Teen Club kids Christmas caroling last Friday night, and we had such fun. The Hamiltons had prepared ice shavings to throw at us to make us think that it was winter. (The temperature was 89° F at 7:30 PM. This afternoon, we had the Bible Club Christmas party. Thursday morning, Jennifer's class has its party, and I have to make the cookies. Friday night, we have all the missionaries here for a Christmas party. Saturday, we have the English Chapel party, and then, the next Tuesday night, we have our churches special Christmas Service. All of these are in our home, and I have to make goodies for them all. I just found out that there will not be any meat in the city until after the first of the year, and so, we will be meatless until then. How do you fix a turkeyless Christmas dinner? So far we have sixteen people that we know for sure will be coming for Christmas dinner, in addition to our family.

Robert just came in and a patient has given him a live turkey, so that takes care of Christmas dinner. The only problem is that it is so skinny that I will have to slice it very thin to go around. The home-grown turkeys here do not have double breast; in fact, they are very pointed and have little meat. They are also usually tough. I inject them with wine and butter to try to tenderize them and make my own butterball turkeys.

Mike and Charles are busy making a rabbit hutch. A friend gave the kids two rabbits. Now we have a menagerie consisting of a boa constrictor (6' 5" long and 7" in diameter), a duck, two rabbits, a cat, a dog, and a macaw. Charles and his friend rescued the boa that someone had tried to kill by putting a stick through its neck. He knows that I hate snakes, but he promised to build a huge cage in the back where I would not see it. I told him that if I ever caught it outside the cage that it would be a dead snake. The boys have caught rats to feed the snake, but it won't eat. They went to the market and bought some small chicks, but again, the snake wouldn't eat. We think that its throat has scar tissue and it can't swallow …

* * * *

Robert went to Guatemala in 1976 to help with the Earthquake disaster. He was gone for three weeks, and I tried to continue with some of the work that we had started. The mission furnished us with a house and transportation. We had a twelve-seat Chevy van that was lemon in color and in action. Something was always wrong with it. I was transporting twelve people from our church to our mission in a fishing village when a very strong cross wind blew the hood of the car up and smashed it into the windshield. No one was injured, but we were covered in slivers of glass. We were only about ten minutes from the village, so decided to continue on and have our service. The trade winds were blowing so strongly that I was afraid that the whole windshield was going to blow in on us. It normally took us an hour to drive to the village, but coming back I had to drive so slowly that it took us two and a half hours. Our van was only one of two vans in the whole country, and it was difficult to find parts for it. (Our mission had imported the two vans just as we arrived in the country. Most of the cars in Colombia were old model American or Europian made small vehicles.) In Bogotá, which was an hour flight but thirteen hours by car, we finally found a windshield that would fit. Two of our fellow misionaries traveled to Bogotá and gingerly wrapped the windshield in blankets and carried it in the back seat of their car. I had it installed just before Robert returned from Guatemala.

* * * *

An excerpt from letter to parents February 1976 … Carnival celebrations have just begun, and it is getting wilder every minute. Last night, a man was dancing in the street around midnight (drunk) and backed into the path of a car. He broke both arms and both legs. Another night, the brothers Maravillas, well known criminals, were racing down the street, riding double on a motorcycle after robbing several families at gun point. A bus driver was speeding his empty bus down another street after leaving a party. They collided at an intersection, and the brothers Maravillas went flying, killing them both. The witnesses were angry with the drunk driver, and were ready to lynch him, until the police arrived and told the crowd what the brothers had done. The drunk driver then became the hero.

As you know Robert is in Guatemala helping with the earthquake disaster. We just heard that the hospital where he was working collapsed. They had evacuated into a park shortly before, so no one was hurt. We had fifteen teenagers descend on us for Mike's 15th birthday. They ate fifteen extra-large pizzas, two cases of soft drinks, two gallons of home made ice cream and a doubled recipe cake. I made all the pizzas; I froze the crust, the night before so all we had to do was put the sauce and toppings on them and pop them into the oven. (There were no fast food restaurants during our first ten years in Colombia)

Jennifer lost her second tooth and she was very disappointed when the Tooth Fairy forgot to come. Barbara, smart girl, went to the phone and dialed the Tooth Fairy directly (with Jennifer's eyes getting bigger and bigger) and told him that Jennifer was upset with him and when could she expect him to arrive. Barbara assured the fairy that she would tell Jennifer that he would come that very day. Needless to say, Jennifer was very impressed. The Tooth Fairy was at that moment entering Jennifer's room ...

* * * *

An excerpt from letter to parents June 1976: ... Wednesday morning, through someone's carelessness, a big storage tank of diesel oil was dumped at the entrance of the water supply to the aqueduct. Needless to say, it gummed up the water works, the bottled water plant, and the coke bottling plant. Before they announced the incident, people were able to smell the diesel coming out the taps. They shut the water off to the whole city until Monday. Fortunately for us, that was the weekend we took a group of twenty-six teens on a retreat out to the camp in Galapa, and they have their own water well.

Mike started working at the clinic as an orderly and, in general, all-around flunky. He transports patients to and from surgery and x-ray. He helps lift patients, does errands for everybody and helps wherever he can. Dr. George Kollmar had a patient who was a quadriplegic that had a terrible bed sore on his buttocks. George asked Mike to help him clean the big ulcerated area; he then went into detail explaining what they were doing, why and how it happened, and how to prevent it. In describing it to me that afternoon, Mike kept saying how awful it looked, and it was so deep that you could see the bone. I asked him if he got sick.

He said no, but his knees got so rubbery that he didn't think he could stand on them. He had to hang onto the bed.

Charles discovered a volleyball net that he had made and somehow misplaced. He used fishnet knots (that Uncle Harry had taught him in making a seine) to make the net and then ran a nylon cord through the top and bottom. The kids set it up in the back yard, and it works as well as any you could buy. That kid is so creative....

* * * *

Robert was a board-certified surgeon, a member of the American College of Surgery, and had been in private practice in Lake Jackson, Texas for almost six years, but he had to get his medical license in Colombia before he could practice medicine there. To do this, he had to present all of his professional papers going back to his university transcripts and have them all translated by the official translator, (there was only one), notarized by the institution that they came from and by the Colombian Consulate, and then presented to the Ministry of Health in Colombia. They were examined, and next, Robert had to take the medical exams, as if he had just finished medical school, and then be interviewed by a board of Colombian medical examiners. He passed all of this with flying colors, and subsequently had to work for a year for the Government doing rural medicine (similar to the internship that he had done fourteen years before) in order to obtain his license to practice medicine in Colombia. He did his *año rural** (year of rural medicine) in a little pueblo which is a forty-five minute drive from our home. The road was narrow and was constantly under construction, and there were a great many accidents. Each morning, as he was leaving Barranquilla, there was a police officer standing on the side of the road hitchhiking to work in the pueblo where Robert was going, so Robert picked him up, and they became friends. This gave him a little security and helped him get through check-points without any hassle. The clinic provided Robert a jeep to drive to the pueblo so that I would not be without transportation each day.

That was a difficult year for all of us. Every ten days, Robert had to stay three days and nights in the hospital in the pueblo called Sabanalarga where he took emergency room call. He learned a lot that year about the people, the language and the culture. He left at 5:30 each morning, and did not return home until after dark each day. Many of his colleagues asked him why he was doing all this "Mickey Mouse" work when he had a practice in the States, which to them was "Mecca," and could have made more money doing one surgery a month than he made here in an entire month working 24/7. This opened up the opportunity for him to talk about the Lord. He felt that God had given him so much, and that he needed to share this with the people of Colombia. He was able to use his medical skills to help the people physically, and able to use his spiritual gifts to share Christ in a special way. Money was not the issue. Obedience to God was the most important objective. We all love to spend money when we have it. But when you are obedient to God, He changes your wants so that you do not miss what you had before. He provided for our every need, and we never lacked for necessities.

While Robert was doing his *año rural*, I had to run the household, take care of the four children, getting them to and from school and other activities, and all of this in a language that I was still struggling with. The children all started school at different hours of the day, but they all came home to eat lunch, and then returned to school for the afternoon. I was learning how to pay bills, which all came on different days, and had to be paid at different banks at different times.

I had to relearn how to cook and to shop using the products and produce that were available. I learned that I could survive without paper towels and aluminum foil. There were no mixes, frozen foods, instant foods, and many of the spices that I used were not available. Wire coat hangers, pecans, peanuts, salad dressings, and milk products such as sour cream, cottage cheese, whipping cream were not to be found. We could buy ice cream, but it was taseless and no one liked it. We had ice cream freezers and made our own delicious home-made ice cream.

At that time I went to the "super marker" to buy staples. You never knew what would be available so you had to stock up on sugar, flour, etc. Sometimes you had to go to two or three super markets to get an item needed that was not available at the first store. I went to the bakery for bread products, to an open market for my fruits and vegetables, and to the meat market for the meat. I could not stock up on meat to store in the freezer because I never knew when the electricity would go off and everything in the freezer would spoil.

Fast foods were unheard of. I cooked our own hamburgers and pizza. When we arrived in Barranquilla and went to a restaurant, the kids were excited when they saw "hamburger" listed on the menu. The expression on their faces when it arrived was hilarious. The hamburger consisted of two slices of dry white bread with a large meat ball in between.

I learned to adapt my old recipes and learned new ones. We enjoyed the challenges and the new tastes. We made our own potato chips, and our "fritos" were made from thinly sliced plantains that we fried.

I bought unpasteurized milk by the bowl full from an unrefrigerated milk truck. By the time it reached our home in the afternoon (when the temperature was in the upper 90's), it was often clabbered. After a few years, I was able to buy milk in plastic bags in the super market. It was an improvement, but if we didn't consume it in a day, it went bad. I learned to cook with powdered milk, but the children never liked to drink it. They would guzzle milk when we visited another city where there was good milk.

Whenever anyone came from the States, we always asked them to bring special items with them like my favorite spices, peanut butter, etc. One year, someone brought us several boxes of Kraft Macaroni and Cheese. We wrapped them up and gave them to the children for Christmas. They were as excited as if it had been a bicycle. When you don't have the big things, you learn to appreciate the little things.

Years later, Barbara was asked by a group of teens if she missed living in the States. She answered, "Yes, I missed a lot of things. I missed not having T.V. to watch. I missed not having Dr. Pepper or good milk to drink, Snickers to eat, McDonald's hamburgers and fries. I missed not being able to see family and friends, the activities available here. We talked about these things and drooled over the thought of eating and doing everything. Then when we got back to the States, we pigged out on all the food and drinks, got bug eyed watching T.V., visited family and friends; we did a lot of things. Then we began missing Colombia, the foods that we ate there, the friends, the activities. We decided that we would enjoy what was available where we were, knowing that was where God wanted us to be, doing what He wanted us to do. We look forward to what He had for us in the future." *We did not have T.V. for the first ten years we were in Colombia.*

A friend of ours brought a portable dish washer to Colombia, but quickly discovered that the water was too dirty and would clog the hoses and filters.—If—there was water and—if—there was enough water pressure, then more than likely, there would be—no—electricity. The washer became a storage bin and a butt of jokes.

You learn to be flexible. You board buses or taxis that break down, wait for people who never arrive, make cultural and language blunders, and work with people with whom you don't always agree. You take on too much, give and do not receive, and become spiritually dry. I read somewhere that the situation depends on two things:

1. A teachable heart
2. God's Grace.

His grace will be there; but will my heart be teachable? You have to learn your own limitations—physical, mental, spiritual—and realize that you can't "stock up on God's strength"; but you need it each day, each hour. Isaiah 40 tells us to

"Wait upon the Lord and gain new strength." If I depend on God to guide me, I'd better have a teachable heart.

We never regretted our decision to pull up stakes and move to Colombia. Many thought we were making such a big sacrifice, but we never felt that it was a sacrifice. We had the peace and reassurance that this was what God's Will was for our lives. Sometimes we would get discouraged, but He always showed us that we were where He wanted us to be, doing what He wanted us to do. One day, Robert came home upset because a patient had died. Many patients came to him after seeing other doctors and spending all their money, and they expected Robert to preform miracles. It was often too late, and nothing could be done. He was frustrated at some of the poor care that they had received. With this last death, he wondered if God was trying to tell him that it was time to go back to the States. The next day, a patient arrived for a post-operative check-up, and she was all excited and beaming. She said that she had come in not only for the post-op check-up, but she wanted to invite him to her baptism. She and seven members of her family were going to be baptized as a direct witness of the care that she had received from him and the clinic. God was and is so faithful in reconfirming His call for our lives.

* * * *

An excerpt from letter to parents August 1976: ... We finally repaired the water tanks on top of the house. We had to replace the check valves to keep the water from running out into the street. The city water goes off every day, and we need the reserve tanks in order to have some water in the house. The kids have learned how to conserve water. When the city water is off, they do not flush the potties every time they go to the bathroom, and when taking a bath, they use the barrels of water and a gourd to sponge off while standing in the shower.

Around 4:30 Saturday morning, Mike and Charles came up to our bedroom and said that their room was a swimming pool. Sheba, the dog, had tried to jump into bed with Mike, and when he reached down to lift her up, she, along with all the covers, books and everything else that was on the floor, was sopping wet. The city water was off as usual Friday night when we had forty teens here for the weekly Teen Club. One of the teens had evidently gone into the bathroom and turned on the faucet and forgot to turn it off when there was no water. Somehow a washrag had stopped up the lavatory, and when the water came back on during the night, it overflowed like Niagra Falls. There was about three inches of water in the boys' bedroom. There is a drain in the bathroom, but it is the high point of the floor, and we had to sweep uphill to remove the water. It took the three of us two hours to sweep most of the water out, pick up all the wet linens and towels, and put everything out to dry.

Robert was unable to help us with the flooding because he had come home from Sabanalarga with a mild case of hepatitis. For several days, he had been feeling extremely tired; then, he started aching all over and had a low grade fever. He kept working until Thursday when he dragged himself up the stairs to the bedroom and asked me to look at his eyes. They were yellow and his urine was very dark. He went to bed, and the kids, Elena (our maid) and I went to the clinic to take gamma globulin shots to prevent us from coming down with it. Other than being very tired and achy he is doing fine.

Robert had planned on taking Charles fishing for his birthday, but was unable to go, so a dentist friend and another doctor took him. They didn't catch anything, but had a great time.

The last three nights, we have had the worst lightening storms that I have ever seen, and the thunder shook the house. Saturday, the old Poinciana tree in front fell down and squashed our neighbors' little red VW Bug that was parked beneath it. Fortunately, no one was hurt. So that the insurance would pay for their car, our neighbor asked us to tell the insurance people that the tree fell during an earthquake. We don't have earthquakes here. I don't know how they thought the insurance people would accept without challenging that ...

* * * *

Receiving packages from home sometimes posed problems. Robert's aunt always sent us a Collins Fruitcake for Christmas. None of us are fond of fruitcake, but it was nice to serve to company, of which we had plenty. One year, it was mailed in November, but we received it in April of the next year. When customs opened it, a green cloud escaped the canister. The can had been damaged in transit, and inside, there was nothing but dusty, green mold. Another time, my mother sent the children special candy for Easter. It was a long time in arriving, and the rats had left droppings inside the box, so we had to throw everything out.

* * * *

To be a medical missionary a person needs to be flexible and have a love for people and a good sense of humor. I am a registered nurse and my husband is a surgeon. As director of Clinica Bautista in Barranquilla, Colombia, he had an active practice in the clinic, but also went on four to five medical caravans during the year. We would stay from one to two weeks at each place. We began our mobile medical clinics, or medical caravans as we called them, when we first arrived in Colombia because Robert could not practice medicine in a hospital setting until he obtained his medical license. (It took him three years to obtain his license.) We could work in rural areas where there was little to no medical care available. The purpose of the caravans was two-fold: to share the gospel through evangelistic services, and to give medical care to people who had little or no medical attention.

Working in the caravans takes us to all parts of Colombia, each area distinctive in its culture and conditions. The Llanos (Eastern plains) consists of ranch land. We travel for miles without seeing another human. Upon arrival at our destination, pueblo children are sent in all directions by horseback to tell of our arrival. The people come on foot or by horse to be treated and to stay for the evangelistic service held each night. Those who can't return home that night hang their hammocks up in any available space to sleep.

Another area that we travel to is the Chocó, located on a riverbank deep in the jungle where Colombia borders Panama. The six thousand plus residents of the La Loma area live up and down the Bojayá river. They are mostly descendants of African slaves, brought in by the Spaniards during the colonial times, to build walls to fortify the city of Cartagena; but there are also some Embera Indians. Besides La Loma, there are several other small villages along the river in the Chocó that we visit. Other areas are: the Guajira (Northern desert area where the *Wayu** Indians live), the Sierra Nevada Mountains where the *Kogi** and the *Arawak* Indians live, Sucre (interior ranching and farming area where most of the people live along banks of rivers or creeks). The people are all different and each has their own culture, and each of the Indian tribes has its own language.

We gain respect for these people as we experience with them, for a short time, the hardships that they face all year-round: intense heat, high humidity, mud, mosquitoes, no electricity, constantly encroaching jungle, and the nearest medical care several hours up or down the river. These people are poor in material goods and comforts, but rich in spirit and love. They are hungry for the gospel, and we are able to fill that hunger.

We take medicines, surgery equipment, and our clothes and personal items. Items needed are repellant, umbrellas, boots, sun screen, swim suits (for bathing), soap, towels, sheets, a pillow (very important), and hammocks. It depends on the season as to what we take because each area is distinct.

The difference that we can see after several years of going and the satisfaction of helping people that are destitute is thrilling. The poverty is impressive. We take interns and volunteers, doctors, nurses, dentists, health care workers, gofers, pastors, everyone who goes must pull his own weight.

In the Llanos, the transportation is by car in the dry season. We have to ford several rivers and go across country that has no roads. We have to take a guide to help find the trail. We spend a lot of time repairing our cars that break down on the rough terrain. The people there are cowboys that live on the plains and tend their cattle. There is no electricity. Once, they killed a calf for us on the first day and cooked the ribs on an open fire. The next morning, for breakfast, they served the boiled head of the calf complete with horns, whiskers, tongue and eyes staring back at you. I looked at it, and it looked at me, and I just cut a piece of the tongue and passed it on. They salted the rest of the meat to preserve it, and by the fourth day, our gums were so sore and bleeding from eating so much salt that we had difficulty chewing. When we returned to the city, all we wanted to eat was soup or mashed potatoes—nothing that needed to be chewed.

The pigs slept along-side us. We had to go to the well to wash our clothes and hang them on the barbed wire fence. The bathroom was behind whatever bush that you chose. One day, I carried on a conversation with a blind man while I was in the "bathroom" with a severe bout of diarrhea. We had removed a huge lipoma from the man's head earlier that day. Unable to see, and using only a cane, it amazed me how easily he could travel the rough trails. I had not realized that the trail was just beyond my bush. Your sense of modesty is modified in these circumstances.

* * * *

In Sucre, our travel depended on the season. In the dry season, we drove on levies, over plowed fields, and crossed streams and rivers on ferries that are made by putting two dugouts together and nailing planks over them. They do not look very stable. They then pole or pull the ferry by a cable to the other side. In the wet season, we drove to San Marcos, left our cars, and then traveled in dugout canoes for seven or more hours to get to Miraflores.

* * * *

To reach the Kogi Indians on one side of the mountain, we drove to Valludupar, then took an open jeep taxi to where the road ended. Bob Moyer, a missionary with South American Missions (SAM) met us with mules and horses to climb the mountain where he and his family lived and worked. One year, we took our children with us, and we spent New Year's Eve with the Moyers. Jennifer was only seven at that time so we put her on the mule with Robert and tied her to his backside with a *ruana**. The trail was very steep, narrow, rocky, and winding up the mountainside. Everything was going well until the saddle strap under the mule's tail broke. The mule stumbled, and Robert and Jennifer went flying off. That was the only spot on the trail that was not covered with big boulders and rocks. God was truly looking out for them.

While we held clinics during the day, the children played with the Kogi children, and it is amazing how children can communicate without speaking each others' language. One of the children tied a bare branch onto his head and was the bull. The others had huge leaves that were capes and they were the bull fighters. They had a wonderful time.

The Kogis are one of the most traditional tribes in South America, and as such, are of interest to many outsiders. This outside pressure has made many Kogis very unhappy. This pressure has been very difficult for the believers; they often have been kidnapped and forced to practice Kogi rites. Some believers are told they must renounce Jesus or give up their land and leave the tribal area. They want freedom of religion.

To get to the Kogi tribes on the other side of the mountain, we were flown in a small plane piloted by Tom Smoke, a Wyclliff missionary. Tom flew a Heliocourier, which is one of the few planes that could land on the small grass landing strips up in the mountains. He told us the plane could land and take off on a dime.

Each area was different and distinct. They were all big adventures, some more so than others.

*   *   *   *

An excerpt from letter to Pat and D.O. Foster August 1976: ... Tell the sweet children of VBS thank you for their love gift. The Spanish mission church where we have been attending the past two years has been in a building program. They have been meeting in the small back yard of a home with a temporary roof and one wall (the cement wall surrounding the yard). When we began attending, there were about fifty members and now there are somewhere around two hundred. Little by little they have built a new sanctuary and have the walls and roof put up, but ran out of money for the floor. These people are very poor. They gave sacrificially, peso by peso. Sometimes they would put a two peso bill in the offering plate and take out one peso change. (A peso today equals twenty-two cents). With the love offering of the children, they were able to buy the cement and the men are mixing and pouring the floor. We will be able to begin services in the new building by Christmas ...

*   *   *   *

An excerpt from letter to Marcie and Gerald, October 1976: ... We had a little excitement in our clinic a couple of weeks ago. Someone threw a military, fragmentary grenade into a patients room and seriously injured the patient and his wife. He died a week later from infection of his original wounds. He was a big politician, very wealthy and influential. He had a fight with his cousin or nephew, killing him, and in the process received a bullet wound through his eye. They think this latest incident was a revenge action by the family of the first victim. The explosion pretty much destroyed the room, knocking the lavatory off the wall. All the windows and doors to the room were blown out, including the air conditioner. It also blew a crater in the floor. The wife was partially protected by the mattress, as the grenade landed under her bed but she still received some twelve to fifteen shrapnel wounds. There was general panic and confusion, but fortunately, there was no oxygen anywhere near or it could have been a major tragedy ...

*   *   *   *

In 1976, we were planning on twenty-five people for Thanksgiving dinner and each person was bringing a dish. The U.S. Navy came to our rescue and brought us ingredients that we needed. The Navy Chaplain, Dave Hunsicker, who was a Baylor classmate of Robert's, arrived on a Navy tender that docked in Cartagena. They came to work on the Colombian Navy ships and were here until late December. They brought the clinic an x-ray machine that had been donated. Robert and I met them in Cartagena, and they treated us royally. The ship was a floating fix-it shop and fascinating. There were seven hundred sailors on board. They offered to come to Barranquilla to repair anything at the clinic or in our home that needed fixing. They sent six fellows, and they all spent the night at our house and came back the next weekend to do more work. They would not let the kids give up their beds for them, so we separated the mattresses from the box springs, and some slept on a mattress and some on the box springs. The next morning, Elena called me into the back bedrooms giggling and showed me their beds. They were made up ship-shape. You could probably have bounced a coin off the sheets. Their shoes were lined up, and everything was neat as could be. They got up and helped make breakfast and mopped the floors before they left for the clinic. One of the guys was a cook, and when he saw my kitchen and pantry, he was appalled at the quality of some of our ingredients. He called my cooking oil "Axel grease." I had to admit that it was green-colored, but it really did not taste too bad. The next time that they came, they brought me ten lbs. of peanut butter, three boxes of cornmeal, a case of cottonseed oil, and many other items.

* * * *

An excerpt from letter to parents January 1977: ... The entire months of November and December we had company. The beds wouldn't have time to get cold before someone else arrived. On top of that, my washing machine broke down. The Sears maintenance department told me that since the washer was bought in the States, that they had to order the parts from there, and they have a five-month backlog. I had to find someone here to jerry-rig it so that we did not have to wash everything by hand in the *pila**. Happiness is hearing the washing machine run after two months of silence.

We had twenty people here from 8:00AM until 9:30PM on Christmas Day. The kids had as much fun selecting presents for everyone as they did in receiving them. We didn't spend nearly as much this year as we have in the past, but everyone was so pleased with what they gave and what they received. Barbara spent two and a half months making all her gifts. She made a table cloth for the card table using liquid embroidery to paint a beautiful border of morning glories all around it. She monogrammed some handkerchiefs for Mike and painted a frog on some for Charles.

On New Year's Eve we went up into the Sierra Nevada Mountains for a few days. It was gorgeous, and the weather was perfect—cool but not too cold. The bright red poinsettias were in full bloom and were as tall as the houses. The road (if you could call it that) was full of boulders, and it took two hours to travel thirteen miles straight up the mountain side. We were in a jeep and were bounced and tossed around so much that about half way up Jennifer fainted. Once we arrived, it was worth all the difficulty. We stayed in a primative cabin in the middle of a field of coffee. There was a steep, cement coffee bean slide (that the farmers used to convey their sacks of coffee beans from the top of the mountain, down to where it could be transported by burros) and that we all used as a giganic slide to play on. We had a great time just doing nothing but enjoy the scenery and hiking ...

* * * *

In the late 1970's, someone came from the states to give our clinic an evaluation and accreditation. The new Government University Hospital was opening at that same time, and the evaluation of our clinic stated that this hospital would put our clinic out of business within five years. The government hospital was beautiful and expected to be the answer to good, inexpensive medical care for everyone. In reality, within four months of its opening, they were calling our clinic to borrow basic items such as syringes, I.V. solutions, and much more because their equipment had been stolen. We noticed the first and most important qualification of the Minister of Health was always his political affiliation and not his qualification for the job. Corruption almost wiped out the hospital. It is only a shell of its promising beginnings.

* * * *

An excerpt from letter to parents January 1977 ... Since Christmas, Robert has brought home four live turkeys, one hen and one rooster. Patients give them to him when they don't have money to pay for services rendered. Robert brought the rooster home last Thursday, and it crowed all night long. Dr. and Mrs. James Harris from Fort Worth had arrived the night before. (He was our pastor when we were in Seminary and now is president of the Foreign Mission Board). In the middle of the night, I chased the turkey with a tennis racket, and it hushed for about an hour, but started up again. The next day we ate rooster gumbo. Dr. Harris thought that was one of the funniest stories on his trip ... I really appreciate the butterball turkeys that you buy in the States. I have to kill and clean all of our turkeys. The last two turkeys were all feathers, skin and bones. They were so full of pin feathers that I just said, "the devil with them" and cooked them pin feathers and all and then skinned them to eat

Barranquilla has had a serious problem with public water. We were completely without water for four days, and now the water comes on at 4:00AM and goes off at 10:00 or 10:30AM. The pressure is so weak that sometimes it doesn't reach the shower. I keep a barrel filled with water in each of the bathrooms so that we can have bath water and water to flush the potties. I use a hose connected to an outside faucet to help fill the washing machine so it won't strain the machine too much. As soon as the first load is through the wash cycle, I stop the washer and hand-wring the clothes and put them into a big tub. Then I wash another load of clothes in the same wash water. When the second load goes through the rinse cycle, I stop the washer before it drains, hand-wring those clothes dry and put the first load back in to rinse. When it goes through the spin cycle, I put the other load in. You have to conserve as much as possible. The city was without gas and gasoline during the same week. People were lined up for blocks to get gasoline if there was any. The electricity also was going off for several hours each day. The fourth day of the water being off, I awoke with a start at 3:30AM and immediately realized that the water had come on because I could hear air in the pipes. I jumped up and flushed all the potties, which were pretty rank, and scrubbed them. I took a bath and washed my hair and started filling the washing machine with the hose. I got everyone up and made them all bathe and shampoo their hair. I didn't know if or when the water would go off again, and I wanted everyone clean ...

*   *   *   *

An excerpt from letter to Phoebe (my sister) April 1977 ... We were all invited to a *finca** for dinner Sunday and were treated royally. They fed us *Sancocho de gallina**, *arroz con verduras** and *agua de panela** (chicken soup, rice and vegetable, and a drink made of raw brown sugar, water and lemon). They had a horse and a burro to ride. Charles tried riding the burro astride like a horse six times, but that old burro was stubborn. He put his head down to eat, refusing to move, almost making Charles fall off. Mike went out and led, or rather pulled, the burro that Charles was on, around by a rope. The seventh time, Charles left and was gone for about an hour. We were all getting a little concerned and thinking about looking for him when we heard him yell to open the gate at the cattle pen. He came swaggering in looking like a true Colombian. He had his legs crossed over the burro's neck like the farmers here ride, and he was in complete charge. He had mastered the burro. He said it was more comfortable cross-legged, he had the burros' head pulled up by the halter and tied to the saddle so he couldn't lower his head, and he had a stick to tap the animal's rear to make him go. The people there laughed till they cried saying he was truly a *campecino**. When he got off, it was really funny because he looked like he was drunk; his legs were so shaky that he could hardly walk.

Next weekend, we take our teen club on a three-day retreat to our camp in Galapa. We have an average of forty teens that come. I am busy trying to buy food and to coordinate everything.

Robert is preparing a mobile clinic in May to the Chocó, the jungle area on the Colombian border with Panama. I would love to go, but I don't want to leave the kids so much ... Jennifer (age 5) is driving us crazy. She is learning to read, and she is continually sounding out words that she sees. The trouble is she reads in Spanish and sometimes the results come out funny. The other day, we were all in the car, and she read "hey-ahns" and wanted to know what that meant. We couldn't figure out what she was saying until she pointed to a girl on the street and said, "The word on that girl's shirt." Well we all laughed, the word was Jeans, and she had sounded it out phonetically correct in Spanish. She is the only *gringa** in her class, and all the rest speak Spanish.

*　　*　　*　　*

In the first caravans, we were feeling our way, trying to see just what we could do. Robert pulled teeth (something that he dislikes very much and feels unqualified doing). He did minor surgery and a lot of general medicine treating patients with everything from headaches to malaria, to typhoid and everything in between. In the llanos, a ranching area in the Eastern plains, he pulled teeth in the morning. One boy about eleven years old, came to have a tooth pulled and fell off his horse, so we had to set his broken arm before we pulled his tooth. In the afternoon, we did surgery and general medicine and then had to ride horseback into "the boondocks" to deliver a baby later in the day. We were later able to recruit dentists to do the dental work and family practice or other specialties to care for the other needs so that we could do more surgery.

We had to carry all our medicines and surgical equipment with us. The nearest drugstore sometimes was nine hours or more by horseback or canoe.

*　　*　　*　　*

Alejandro was carried into our clinic in a hammock. He had not been able to urinate for eight days, and his abdomen was so distended it looked to be nine months' pregnant. We had forgotten to pack a catheter, but word went out down the river and someone brought us one. We sterilized it and tried to insert it, but Alejandro was so obstructed that it wouldn't pass. Robert made a small incision in the abdomen and inserted a miniset I.V. administration tube directly into the bladder and sutured it to the skin. We showed Alejandro how to take the top off every thirty minutes or so to drain his bladder. He could have gone into shock if it were drained too rapidly. By the end of the day, he was able to walk around. He wanted us to operate on him there, but we explained that he needed major surgery in a hospital setting. This was our first day in Miraflores, and we planned to be there for eight days. Alejandro left the next day. When we arrived in Barranquilla, Alejandro was waiting for us at the clinic ready for his surgery. He had made the seven hour canoe ride to San Marcos, then the fourteen hour bus ride to Barranquilla to get his surgery. He had cancer of the prostate, but was able to receive relief and lived seven years more. He was always the first one to greet us and hug us when we returned to Miraflores.

* * * *

Vaccination was a very important part of our early ministry. There were many cases of polio, tetanus, whooping cough and measles when we first arrived. While holding a vaccination clinic in a small fishing village, I thought that I was getting a repeat of children being vaccinated. It was hard to think that a child would voluntarily return to get another injection. We vaccinated more than nine hundred children that day so it was hard to recognize all those children. I investigated and found that a group of eleven and twelve year-olds where gathering the smaller children, bathing them, putting clothes on them, and then bringing them to be vaccinated. Then they collected other children, bathed them, and dressed them in the same clothes that had been on the first group, and brought them to the clinic. I was recognizing the clothing, not the children. They did this all day. The children in this village normally do not wear clothing until they begin school. I was very impressed with the older children who cared enough for others to make sure that they were protected from these diseases.

* * * *

An excerpt from letter to Pat and D.O. Foster, June 1977 ... I am sitting on a mountain roadside with my feet in a running cold mountain stream. I have been sitting here for four hours. We started on our vacation yesterday, and this morning, we got caught by a big mud slide that closed the only road to Medellín. There is a line of cars two miles in front of us, and I hate to think how far behind. I believe I could live the rest of my life in Latin America and never understand their thinking. Cars, trucks, and buses are all sure that they can get through the long line of traffic stalled here. Now there is a Mexican standoff with at least three lanes of traffic on either side of the mud slide on a narrow road that is barely wide enough for two lanes with a sheer drop off on one side. When the area is opened, there will still be no where to go. Fortunately, we stopped for breakfast this morning in a café that did not serve breakfast, as we know it, so we all ate steak and potatoes. We have cokes cooling in the stream. I have crackers, peanut butter and bananas in the car, and Charles went down the road and bought a dozen oranges. At least we won't go hungry. It is interesting to talk to the people and watch their reactions to the circumstances. Fortunately, the weather is nice and the four kids are not cooped up in the car but can get out and play with the other children around …

* * * *

Jim Oliver had donated an old portable pump organ to be used by the mission. We used it in the English-speaking service as well as in various missions. For me, pumping with my feet while playing the keyboard was like patting my head and rubbing my stomach at the same time. In the fishing village of La Isla, I had a three-legged stool to sit on while I was playing. As I would pump the organ, which was sitting on sandy ground, it kept moving away from me, and I would have to scoot the stool to keep up with the organ. It was pump, scoot, play, pump, scoot, play.

Robert was always having to maintain the organ to keep it in working order. He frequently had to clean the splinters out of the pipes. He used the elastic on his undershorts to repair the bellows that broke. We had a volunteer visiting us and she was horrified. She wrote to our area director and told him that he needed to do something to help those poor missionaries in Colombia. "Dr. Edwards had to use his underwear to repair their pump organ." Dr. "Breezy" Brasington, our area director, took care of that problem in his usual sensible way. He sent Robert a set of new underwear. We eventually donated the organ to a mission in Valledupar that was being organized into a church.

Chapter 2

A Buena Hambre, No Hay Mal Pan

(If you're hungry, any food will taste good)

Mike graduated from high school when we were on furlough in Houston, Texas in 1978. Leaving him was one of the hardest things that we had to do when we returned to Colombia in June of that year. He was going to major in chemistry at Houston Baptist University. He later switched to pre-med.

* * * *

An excerpt from letter to Mike September1978 … Thieves broke into the house early Monday morning and wiped us out. Our crates had been delivered that week, and we were still unpacking. I heard them, and we don't know if I scared them off or if they had already taken everything out the window that they wanted. All the new things that we were looking forward to using and wearing for the next four years were stolen. We were all upset at our losses until that afternoon the tragedy at the Hotel Prado pushed all thoughts of our robbery out of our mind.

The commercial annex to the Hotel was a seven-story building on one side of the hotel. They had the columns up, and the cement floors were all poured.

When they removed the stick supports (remember how they used tree limbs for support instead of metal) the whole structure collapsed. No one knows, or at least no one admits, what went wrong, but it is thought that someone mixed more sand than cement into the mixture. They eventually recovered twenty-two bodies and then pieces of bodies. The stench of putrefying flesh and fumigation became almost unbearable before the week was up. Everyone had to wear masks. Delores Ballard, Joyce Cain and I along with several members of the American Women's Club were there Tuesday through Saturday feeding the rescue workers with food and water donated by many concerned people throughout the city.

There were a lot of Oxygen canisters for the welders, and one fellow was rolling a cannister on the ground when the valve came off, and like a torpedo, with Oxygen spewing everywhere, it headed straight for our food table. Joyce says that she wished she had a movie camera when I jumped our feeding table, and snatched the cigarette out of the mouth of the wife of the American Consulate, ground it out in the sand, and then shoved her out of the way. She has since forgiven me, and in fact, we are eating dinner at their house next week. Joyce teases your Dad about being married to a kid that can hurdle tables. This really was a tragic time for Barranquilla, but everyone united briefly to help in any way that they could. Many stores and bakeries donated food to help feed the rescue workers, people brought us ice and bottled water, and we had hot coffee for everyone.

* * * *

The first few years that we were in Colombia the stretch of road to the fishing village of La Isla was a beautiful peninsula. On one side was the Caribbean Sea, and on the other was a brackish mangrove swamp full of iguanas, monkeys and tropical birds. The road was in terrible condition and was always under repair. In the process of working on the road and elevating it, they neglected to put in drainage culverts so the water could flow from the swamp to the sea. The final blow came when they installed a gas aqueduct along the roadside and completely stopped the flow. In just a few years we had an ecological disaster that will take 100's of years to restore. All of the trees died leaving no home for the wildlife. It looks like an atomic bomb was dropped, leaving everything dead. It affected the wildlife, the fishermen, and the entire ecosystem. They have since gone in and put several culverts along the road, but it was too little too late.

* * * *

An excerpt from letter to Mike October 1978 ... Jeni stayed with the kids while your Dad and I drove to Valludupar, left our car with a Wyclliff couple, and then took a taxi (an old open jeep) up the mountain for three hours until the road ended at Atanques. Bob Moyer met us there with horses and mules, and we rode up narrow mountain trails for another two hours, arriving around 8 PM in Sarachuí where the Moyers live.

The first morning, we went to a Kogi Indian hut where the wife of a Witch Doctor, or *Mama** as they are called, was lying on a pallet. She had a compound fracture of the tibia. They expected her to die and were touching the exposed bone with their dirty hands, to wish her good luck in the life to come. We cleaned up the site trying to avoid infection and immobilized it by putting the leg in a cast. The Witch Doctor had been against the mission work and would not give permission for his people to go to the mission where they dispensed medicine and administered first aid. He was so grateful now that he supports the Moyers in their work. Another Witch doctor from another tribe brought his wife whose legs were covered with warts. After I had washed off all the mud on her feet and legs so that we could see all the warts, Robert was able to cauterize the warts to break up the clusters. The *Mama* waited to see the results of his wife's treatment before bringing in his most prized possession for wart treatment—his dog. The poor dog's face was covered with warts. We did not treat the dog.

Juan was an outcast because he had a big cyst growing out of the side of his eyebrow. He was called "the Horned One." We rigged up an operating table, and I assisted while Bob acted as circulating nurse and held the flash light. Afterwards, we gave the man a mirror to see himself, and he broke down crying. He tried to thank us, but we told him to give God the honor and glory because we were just His instruments. Juan is now living in the tribe as a celebrity.

We really had a lot of satisfying experiences there. Then we had to go down the mountain! I have never been so scared. It had been dark when we went up so I couldn't see how steep it was or how narrow. One leg would brush the side of the mountain, and the other was hanging out over empty space.

Zack and Barbara Deal came for their physicals. Your Dad is doing a hysterectomy on Barbara, and they will stay here for a couple of weeks to recuperate. They will be with us for Thanksgiving. Your Dad had a turkey given to him, as usual, and I had to kill and clean it. It has a little more meat on it than usual.

Is there any chance that you could come for Christmas? I can dream can't I? Charles is making a nine-foot macrame Christmas tree, and it is really something to behold. He has to have it finished before all the Christmas parties start here at the house. We have the Barranquilla missionaries Christmas party here on December 19 …

* * * *

After Christmas Robert and I, plus Barbara, Charles and Jennifer returned to Sarachuí to spend New Years with the Moyers and to hold clinics. We visited with the *Mama*'s wife with the fractured leg. She had refused to go down the mountain to a hospital, so did not heal as well as she could have. It would take a long time for her to be able to walk again, if ever, but she was alive and doing well. The Kogi people were so grateful that they made Robert an honorary Witch Doctor. It seems strange to say that a Baptist missionary doctor was a bona fide Witch Doctor, but stop and think, the *Mama* is the most powerful person in the tribe, and he speaks with the ultimate authority. We now had an entry to preach the gospel with authority and power.

Robert, Barbara, Charles, and Bob M. hiked to a Kogi village to visit with patients. It was a three-hour hike there and three hours back, up and down steep, narrow, twisting mountain paths. On the way back, Robert used Barbara as an excuse to stop and rest often to catch his breath. On one of their stops, a young Kogi Indian, whom we had treated a month before, passed them trotting up the mountain like a mountain goat without even breathing heavily. When we saw him the month before he was "dying" from T.B. His mother had died a short time before from T.B. He arrived at the house where we were staying, and I told him that the doctor wasn't there but should be back shortly. He laughed and said yes, he knew; he had passed them on the trail about an hour before.

* * * *

One day, Robert was in surgery at the clinic when the lights went off in the middle of a case. This was not unusual, and the emergency generator came on immediately. The only problem was that the generator was not powerful enough for the air conditioner to function. With all the surgery garb on—the gown, gloves, mask and cap, and the hot lights—it became extremely hot, and the surgeons and nurses were sweating profusely. Robert looked up at the ceiling and said, "Lord, it sure would be nice to have a cool breeze in here." About that time, he felt a cool breeze around his legs. He looked down, and his scrub pants had fallen to his ankles. The drawstring had broken, and down they went. The nurse ran over to pull them back up and he told her, "No, the Lord had a sense of humor in answering my prayer." They continued with the surgery without any more interruptions, chuckling and saying that you had to be careful what you prayed for.

* * * *

An excerpt from letter to Phoebe (sister) December 1978 ... Robert was a big hit as Santa Claus at the Christmas Bazaar of the American Woman's Club. In Spanish, he is called *Papa Noel*. He had to be bilingual that day because there were scads of kids; half spoke English and the other half spoke Spanish. He had fun, but wouldn't care to do it often ... Robert and I had fun up in the mountains. I wish I could tell you everything that happened. It was like living back in the pioneer days. I had never met the couple who lived there, and she later told me that they were concerned that our trip would be a failure, not knowing us and if we could rough it. We got along beautifully. Their bathroom was either an outhouse or a chamber pot. If you wanted a hot bath, you bathed in a #3 washtub with water heated on a wood burning stove; or if you were brave, you showered outside in the middle of the day in a makeshift shower. The first shower was rather a shock, not only from the water piped from a cold mountain stream, but after being all lathered up covered only by suds, you hear these giggly voices saying *Hunchaka**. (Hello, how are you). The Kogis don't generally take baths and thought it was funny that we did. After that cold water hit me, I could understand why they didn't. It was amazing that they did not have a body odor, but after visiting several of their huts, we understood why. Their huts have mud walls, cone-shaped thatched roofs, no windows and only a low door that you stoop through to enter. They have a fire burning twenty-four hours a day in the middle of the one room dwelling. Upon entering, your eyes burn from the dense smoke. The constant contact with this smoke acts as a natural deodorant. It also irritates the eyes and can cause Pterygium* (an inflammatory growth that sometimes goes from the inside corner of the eye covering the cornea and can cause blindness). We had topical anesthesia, but we didn't have retractors small enough to use to hold the eye lids open. I had a couple of paper clips in my purse, so we bent them into the shape needed, sterilized them, and they worked perfectly. Robert removed the growth and restored vision to several of the Kogi.

One morning we got up early and climbed the hill(?) behind their house—straight up 2,000 feet to a plateau where we ate breakfast and watched the sunrise. We had the most awe inspiring devotional looking down in the valleys and up at the even taller peaks, marveling at God's great creation. Their home is 5,700 feet, so we were around 7,700 feet.

✱   ✱   ✱   ✱

Over the years we have had interesting Christmas trees. The first year we did as the nationals did; we found a large bare limb with several branches, spray painted it white, glued small Styrofoam balls all over it, and put red bows at strategic places all over the tree. It was very attractive. Another year, the family went up into the mountains where a group of men were topping cedar trees. We took one of the cut tops home with us and still had to cut off a good portion to fit into our twelve-foot ceiling living room. It was a true Charley Brown tree. The branches were very sparse, and it was lopsided. It was pathetic-looking, but we loved it. On the 6th of January, we all went to the beach, planning to have a wiener roast and the traditional burning of the Christmas tree. The tree was so dry that it made a "Whoosh" sound and was consumed immediately.

Another Christmas, our son Charles made a nine-foot tall macrame tree that was very interesting. He tied green yarn in macrame knots around wire rings that were graduated in size and hung it from the ceiling. It was easy to store; it just collapsed down into the bottom ring and lay flat. We used that tree for several years, as long as we lived in that house. When we moved to an apartment with much lower ceilings, we gave the tree to one of the churches, and they are still using it.

Christmas time was always very special for us. We made our gifts for one another instead of buying them. Weeks before Christmas, everyone was busy. A lot of giggling and whispering went on behind closed doors. You did not enter a room without knocking and asking permission that sometimes was not granted. We had a box with handkerchiefs or doodads for unexpected Christmas guests. On Christmas Day, all the missionaries in town and many others would gather at our home for an old-fashion Christmas dinner. I cooked the turkey and cornbread dressing, and everyone else would bring a dish. I never knew just how many we would have. Our children would sometimes come home and say, "Mom, I invited so-and-so to come for Christmas dinner. Is that ok?", fully knowing that it was, as long as they let me know so that there would be enough food. The largest gathering that we ever had was fifty-six, and we always had plenty of food. People would come early and stay late, and we always ended the day stuffed and happy, sharing the true meaning of Christmas. In those days, we did not have T.V., so everyone played games or just sat around visiting. We also had a big table with a jigsaw puzzle which was a favorite site for some.

*   *   *   *

It was very important to understand the culture of the people that we treated. Never more so than when we had a fourteen-year-old Embera Indian mother come to our clinic in the Chocó bringing her three-month-old baby. She asks us if our God was powerful enough to save her baby. We were speechless at first and wanted to be very careful how we answered her because if we said the wrong thing, she would either leave her baby in the jungle to die or throw him into the river. After doing a thorough physical on the infant and getting the history, we were able to answer her. The baby had been born three months premature, and the mother had immediately secured it to her breast, binding it with several layers of cloth, giving it constant nourishment and warmth, thereby making a natural incubator. We explained that, yes, our God was a powerful and loving God, and that He had loved her and the child so much that He had given her the wisdom to care for him in possibly the only way that he could have survived. If she continued to look toward God for wisdom in caring for the child, he had a good chance of growing into a young man. She went home very happy.

It is interesting to note that this baby is now a young man. At present, in his village, there is an openness and eagerness to know the Gospel. We don't know for sure, but would like to believe that there is a connection.

Embera Indian mothers. They are fourteen years old, still children themselves.

* * * *

An excerpt from letter to parents September 1979 … There is an epidemic of dengue fever in the city, and Charles and I were two of its victims. The rest of the family is fine. It is spread by mosquitos and not by contact of another person. We had the typical case—high fever for eight days and a rash in the palms of our hands and the bottoms of our feet. They don't call it the "bone breaking fever" for nothing. Every bone in your body hurts, and if you move your eyes, you feel like your head will fall off its perch. We are past that stage, but now we have extreme exhaustion. When everyone left for school and work, Charles came up to lie in bed with me. He said he was bored and wanted to play cards. He dealt out the cards to play two-handed rook and then said, "Lets take a nap and then play the hand." It had taken all his energy to just deal the cards.

Jennifer is wrapped up in the hoola—hoop craze and has become an expert. In the back yard Charles made a fish pond with a waterfall using the cement that Jennifer gave him for his birthday. It is really attractive, and he has landscaped it well, and so far has two goldfish in it. We have a new puppy that is a big ball of fluff. The kids named him Moshe after Moshe Dayan of Israel because they both have an eye patch.

* * * *

Mike was coming home for Christmas, we had not seen him for a year and a half. He called and told us the flight, time and day. We had arranged our schedules to meet him and have as much time to spend with him as possible. The day before he was to arrive, the door bell rang, and Rosemary Kollmar was at the door with a surprise package. She had been at the airport seeing a friend off, and just happened to watch a plane arriving when she recognized Mike deplaning and brought him home. The Lord was looking out for Mike, as he only had fifty cents in his pocket, not enough for transportation from the airport to the house nor the correct coinage for a phone call to let us know he had arrived. He had given us the correct time and flight, but the wrong day.

* * * *

An excerpt from letter to parents June 1980 ... During the past month, there has been an epidemic of polio and gastroenteritis in Barranquilla. In thirty days, one hundred thirty nine kids, all under the age of four, died of gastroenteritis. Twenty more kids died with polio; one hundred fifty more cases were reported. The FMB sent ten thousand doses of polio vaccine. Robert had contacted the local Director of Health Services to expedite getting the vaccine through customs, but the Director was fired from office on the day that the shipment arrived, and it was confiscated by the customs agents. We begged them to keep the vaccine refrigerated so that it would not be damaged until we could get it released, which took about a week. We have since been busy immunizing kids that were at risk. Jeni and her group from ProSalud went into the barrios where there were so much gastroenteritis, and they taught better sanitation practices and how to re-hydrate the kids. There were fewer deaths in these barrios than in the rest of the city.

For lunch today I was planning to fix sloppy joes and french fries. Mike asked if his girl friend could come, and about an hour before lunch, three missionaries with the Wyclliff Mission called and were in town, so they came over. Robert called me to come pick him and Reed up at the clinic. The president of our seminary in Cali was at the clinic, and he came also. Instead of the five that I had planned for, we had thirteen. I cleaned out the refrigerator and made a surprise stew instead of the sloppy joes. You get very creative in instances like this which seem to happen often at our house.

*   *   *   *

The first time we arrived in the Chocó, we were met by the Witch doctor from the Embera tribe. He wanted to evaluate the group. He was happy for us to handle any physical problems that we encountered, but if anyone came to us that had the "evil eye", he would be happy to take over. We found that many people had an amulet around their throat or wrist to ward off the "evil eye." They were also afraid to have their children vaccinated. We finally convinced a good number to bring their children in to be vaccinated against DPT, measles, and polio. When we returned to that area six months later, there was a measles epidemic up and down the river villages, but in the village where we had vaccinated there was not one case of measles. This convinced the people how important prevention was. It was harder to convince them that God was more powerful than the "evil eye".

Robert had to insert a Foley catheter into a man who had difficulty urinating. He injected five cc's of sterile water into the bulb so that it would stay in place, and we taped the catheter to his leg. During the night the man became disoriented and pulled the catheter out, inflated bulb and all. Ouch!

Men in the area complained of back and shoulder pain. Upon questioning, we discovered that they all carried heavy boat motors on their shoulders. The women complained of burning eyes. Almost always we discovered that they cooked over an open fire, and the smoke was irritating their eyes. We never had enough eye drops, vitamins, skin cremes, or pain medication.

*   *   *   *

When we first started going to the Chocó, we were impressed with the honesty of the people. On one trip the pastor, José DeMoya, lost all the money that he had brought. Some time later, it was returned by a young boy who found it lying on the bank of the river where it had fallen out of José's pocket. José was a poor man, and that was a lot of money to him. The young boy was even poorer and could have used it, but he said that it did not belong to him, thus returned it to its rightful owner.

* * * *

An excerpt from Christmas letter 1980 ... We spent the first three months without a drop of water in the house. All water had to be carried in from outside sources. We kept barrels of water in the bathrooms for taking baths and flushing the toilet. We had to conserve water, which was hard when the flow of visitors did not cease.

A couple of interesting and different visitors were Ramon and Vicente, his son, who are Kogi Indians from the Sierra Nevada. They stayed with us for three weeks. Ramon, chief of his village, came to see Robert about a medical problem. Vicente, around seven or eight years old, had never left the mountains before. His adventure into civilization was an education for him and for us. We all throughly enjoyed initiating him into playing softball, sleeping in a bed, using a bathroom, taking a bath, eating with a fork and many other things that we take for granted. He learned very quickly. We were eating hot dogs for lunch and showing Vicente how to eat it. He kept looking at the hot dog on his plate, giggling as he watched our dog running around the table. We said, "No, No not that kind of dog."

They were eager to learn all our "strange ways" and were often giggling about something. At night, they retired early, and we could hear them singing and chanting in their room. Our kids laughingly said that I should check to make sure that they didn't have a fire built in the middle of the room. The room was always dark. Finally, after the third night, I accompanied them to their room, reached in and turned the light switch on. They were so amazed at this magic that they then slept with the light on for several nights. They were delightful guest, and we learned as much from them as they did from us. I prayed that we would be good guest when we went to their village as they had been in our home. Vicente went to the zoo with Robert, and he was so excited about the different animals that he saw in cages, many of which he saw in the wilds of his mountain home. Our children taught him how to play softball and he loved it. He was my shadow. Everywhere I went, he was right beside me. He loved going in the car with me to pick up the kids at school or to go shopping for food. Both Ramon and Vicente wore the typical Indian clothing; a white, cotton tunic that reached mid-calf. Both boys and girls wore this. The boys received white pants to wear under the tunic when they reached puberty. They all wore their hair long. Boys and men wore two *mochilas** crisscrossed over their chest. Girls and women wore red beads. I was often concerned that someone might say something derogatory to them, but this never occurred. Our church accepted them and treated them as special people. Vicente was being groomed to be a "Mama", instead he became a Christian.

We went on four caravans during this year. The Lord is greatly blessing these trips by strengthening existing work and by also opening up new regions. Robert is able to do quite a bit of surgery under primitive conditions in many of these areas.

Nelson, an eleven year-old boy from the Chocó, shattered his elbow, so Robert brought him to the clinic for surgery, and he stayed in our home about three weeks recuperating. Victoria, a twelve year-old girl, was a cripple with a bone infection. With surgery, her leg was straightened and freed of infection, and after a lot of treatment and TLC she is now walking normally.

Alberto S. was considered a very bad hombre and had his neighborhood terrorized. He was a fighter, a mugger, a tough guy, but he came to know the Lord and he is a completely new person. He now is a faithful, dynamic Christian worker. Every Sunday, Alberto brings someone new to church that knew him in his old life, who wants to find out what changed Alberto's life so drastically.

For those of you who donated books for our English library, there are many people here that say "thank you, thank you". It has been very successful. All the books have been read and reread. This has been a big need, not only among missionaries and their children, but also among the English-speaking community....

* * * *

Barbara came home for summer vacation after her freshman year at Baylor in 1981. She was hand carrying a Styrofoam ice chest filled with polio vaccine protected by dry ice. After our experience with customs with the large shipment of vaccine earlier, we didn't know what to expect. We told her to tell the customs agents, if they asked, that it was polio vaccine for the clinic, and that they were going to vaccinate the children in the poor *barrios**. The reaction of the customs agents was to pat Barbara on the back and thank her, wishing that more young people were as caring. You never know what to expect. During her visit, Barbara went with a team to the Chocó to translate for a volunteer dentist. The volunteer continued on to another site, and Barbara traveled back to Barranquilla with Vic Norman and José DeMoya. Vic had not traveled these roads by himself before. He depended on José, the national, to be his navigator. José did not drive but took buses everywhere, so was not really familiar with the roads. They took a wrong turn, and the car broke down out in the middle of nowhere. Vic saw a burro on the side of the road and thought he would catch it and ride into town to get help. Everyone in this area rode burros and it looked simple. After several unsuccessful tries, he decided to walk into town where he did find help. They had to tow the car into town, but since it was Sunday, they had to wait until the next day to have it repaired. They could not call us to let us know that they were delayed because the phones were all down. Vic was very nervous with the responsibility of our daughter and having to stay overnight in what we would call a boarding house. Vic made sure that they had rooms next to each other and told Barbara not to leave her room without letting him know. Even if she had to go to the bathroom at night, she was to knock on the wall and he would walk her to the bathroom which was down the hall. They arrived at our door the next day, hot, tired and dirty; there had been no water where they stayed. We were not worried because we were not expecting them until that day. When I ask how everything went, Vic just grimaced and said "Don't ask me just now." Barbara thought it was a great adventure.

* * * *

Mike and Barbara spent the summer of 1981 in Barranquilla. Since they were both thinking about studying medicine, they wanted to watch their Dad do surgery. They watched a hernia and a gall bladder procedure. Barbara almost fainted and had to sit on the floor with her head between her legs. Mike was so embarrassed, but he wouldn't admit to feeling queasy himself. He later became a perinatologist, which is an obstetrician who treats high risk pregnancy and delivery. Barbara later became an operating room nurse.

* * * *

An excerpt from letter to parents August 1981 ... Mike has fallen in love with a precious Colombian girl named Dunia Chemás. He could not have picked a sweeter, more beautiful girl if he had looked all over the world. She is getting a degree in business administration here at the university and will finish a year from this December. Mike assured Dunia that it wasn't important that she didn't know how to cook, but privately, he told me that it was. He asked if I could teach her before they got married. It is going to be hard on Mike and Dunia this next year and a half with him studying in the States and her studying here.

* * * *

In January, 1982, Mark Klaassen (a medical student from Indiana) and his wife, Sue, arrived for two months study at the clinic. They stayed at our home, and Mark was able to go on one caravan with us to the Llanos. Sue worked as a secretary in the States and was concerned that she might not be able to do anything while they were here. She was a God-send. I had been collecting recipes and trying to put together a cookbook for the mission, but I never seemed to have the time to work on it. Sue spent her time organizing and typing it. She did a wonderful job and was kept very busy.

* * * *

Dr. Vic Norman saw the need of training someone in each village to help with primary health care when there was no doctor. He, along with Jeni Hester, developed the Health Promoter program, revising and adapting the book *Where there is no doctor* to fit the needs in the remote villages. They then chose several people from different villages and pueblos to train in primary health care. These people were also taught how to evangelize. They were great helps to us when we arrived for mobile clinics. They were trained to continue post-op care of patients that had surgery, including the removal of sutures. They could treat vomiting, diarrhea and dehydration that results from these ailments. They could treat minor cuts and injuries, and they knew when to refer the patient to a doctor.

* * * *

Some pueblos were extremely cooperative with the medical caravan team and readily learned and applied the teachings of the team to improve their living conditions. After several years, we have seen a remarkable improvement in their standard of living, sanitation, diet, health, vaccinations, and family planning. There was a marked reduction in deaths due to diarrhea and vomiting.

* * * *

Mike and Dunia were married in a Barranquilla church on December 18, 1982. Barbara was to be the maid-of-honor. Dunia's eighty year-old grandmother, Doña María, made all the bridesmaids gowns. Doña María took Barbara's measurements the year before and told Barbara not to gain any weight before the wedding. In Miami, Barbara was bumped from two different flights while trying to get to the wedding in Barranquilla. Crying, Barbara approached the ticket agent explaining that she had to get to Barranquilla for her brother's wedding. They managed to get her on the next flight. She arrived the evening of the wedding without her luggage, it had arrived the day before and was locked in a storage room at the airport. We didn't have time for them to open the storage room and retrieive her luggage so we hurried home. Mike was pacing up and down the front porch. In his nervousness, he told Barbara not to greet anyone but to get dressed immediately. Fortunately, her dress was at our house and it still fit; we all lent her neccessities, and then rushed to the church. We had called Dunia's home and told her mother what was happening and asked if they could delay fifteen minutes getting to the church. We made it, and the ceremony was only a few minutes late in starting. Mike and Dunia had known each other since they were thirteen and had never had an unchaperoned date before their wedding. There was so much red tape involved in getting married, due to Government regulations, that one of our national pastors, who also was a judge, suggested that they go the route of a proxy marriage. Mike went before a judge in Houston and they were legally married by proxy in October,1982. They celebrate their anniversary in December. Dunia could not get her visa in time to travel back to the States with Mike so she stayed with us when he had to return to go to the university. Robert helped her get her visa, and she lived with us during that time. We were traveling back to the States in mid-January for furlough, and she traveled with us. When we were interviewed by the Foreign Mission Board before appointment, they ask us a question, "What will you do if one of your children wants to marry a national?" Many years later Mike and Dunia were living in Mobile, Alabama, and the pastor of their church was Dr. Drew Gunnels, who had been president of the FMB at the time of our appointment. When I saw him, I said, "I can answer your question now. Mike married a precious Christian girl, and she is a part of the Baptist heritage of Colombia. Her parents are active in the Baptist work of Colombia, and her maternal grandparents worked with the first missionary to Colombia. Some of the first services were held in their home." Dr. Gunnels often used her as "a product of missions" to promote missions in his church.

We furloughed in Houston from January 1983 until June 1984. In August of 1983, the eye of Hurricane Alicia passed over Houston, and everyone was without water and electricity for several days. Our kids put on their bathing suits, stood under the eaves of the apartment complex, and bathed with the rain water rushing off the roof. They also collected this water so that we had a good supply in the house. Our neighbors asked them how they knew to do that. The kids replied that by living in Colombia, where water was often scarce, everyone learned how to use every resource.

Chapter 3

Querer es Poder

(Where there is a will there is a way)

We returned from furlough in June 1984, and we lived out of suitcases until we moved into our apartment. We had left our three older children in the States attending universities and returned with only our youngest child, Jennifer. We did not need as much room so we moved into an apartment about half the size of the house that we had lived in for the first ten years. We had asked the mission to move us because the utility bills had exhausted all our savings; we were paying for utilities that we were not receiving. For weeks, I had spent hours in lines to make complaints trying to get someone to check the electric meter. They finally agreed that no one was reading the meter. In spite of the fact that it was their error, we had to pay or have our power cut off. A neighbor also complained and refused to pay his bill so had his lights cut off. He happened to be an ex-mayor of the city, and it all came out in the headlines of the newspaper along with a picture of him and his family eating by candlelight. The electric company was embarrassed and offered to turn his electricity back on, but the ex-mayor refused unless they corrected the corruption.

There was a lot to be done to our new apartment to fix it up: painting, plumbing, wiring, putting in kitchen and bathroom cabinets, and installing ceiling fans in all the rooms. We had not yet received our crates from the States that contained our new appliances so we washed clothes by hand on a rubboard. We had the loan of an old refrigerator (model 1930) that did not make ice so I had to buy a bag of ice each day. You learn that there are blessings even in the inconveniences. One night, after I had been painting all afternoon and was covered in paint, sweat and dirt, there was no water to bathe. Robert said that the first thing he learned during our first term here was how to bathe, brush his teeth, shampoo his hair, and shave with just one glass of water. I put this to practice that night with the melted ice. If I had not been forced to buy ice, I couldn't have taken a bath.

It took me twenty-five minutes to find the right keys to leave the apartment the first morning that I had to take Jennifer to school. There was one for the back door, one for the *reja** (iron bars), one for the door from the patio to the garage, one for the garage to the outside, and one for the big iron doors from the garage area to the street. That was just getting out the back of the apartment. To enter the front, we needed a key to open the iron railing around the front of the building, a key to open the big glass door to the apartment building, and one to open our front door. Our key chains were rather heavy. For the car, we had a key for the ignition, a different key for the door, a key for the spare tire, a key for the gas tank, a key for the fire extinguisher, a key for the glove compartment, a key for the tire jack, and a key for the Club that locked the steering wheel to prevent theft.

After our experience of such high electric bills in the other house, I was pleasantly surprised at how low the bills were in the new apartment. The third month that we were in the apartment, a meter reader from the electric company rang the doorbell. He had found that our meter had been altered to falsely register our usage and said that they were going to cut off our service and that we would be prosecuted for fraud. I told him that we had just moved into the building and did not know anything about it. I ask him what we needed to do. He said that we needed to get someone to work on the meter so that it would register correctly. When I asked him whom we should get, he said that he could do it. W—ee—ll, I ask him if he would, paid him a fee, and had him sign a receipt with his name and *cedula** (identity card). As soon as I had paid him, he said, "If you would like, I can alter the meter so that no one will be able to detect that it is altered." I just smiled, thanked him, and said no thanks.

* * * *

Years later, when we returned home one night, there was a strong smell of gas. We started looking and found that someone had stolen our gas meter. They had cut the line and the meter from the house and left the line leaking gas. Fortunately, no one had passed by with a lighted cigarette. I called the gas company, and they immediately sent someone to close the line. It took them *only* two weeks to replace the meter. We had them put a metal cage around it with a lock. Another key!

Everything had to be under lock and key, or it disappeared. I even had trees and plants that were stolen. There was a group of young boys who rode burros and mules across the yard, and at mid-day, they would stop under our bedroom window and talk loudly, use the bathroom, and in general, make a mess. They would turn on the outside faucet to get a drink for themselves and their animals and then would "forget" to turn the faucet off. The city water went off every day. We had storage tanks on the roof so that we would still have water inside even when the street water went off, but these boys often drained our tanks. I planted large thorny, cactus like plants all around the front and side of the building to discourage people from stealing the plants and to stop these boys from using my yard for a stable and a bathroom.

*   *   *   *

In 1984, our annual Mission Meeting was held at a rustic YMCA camp in the mountains outside Bogota. Mission meeting was the time when all the missionaries and their families would get together for fellowship, give reports on what was happening, make plans for the next year, and prepare a budget. We always invited some group from the States that came to care for our children while we met. We also had a special speaker that started our day with a devotional message. Often this was the only time that we got to see our fellow missionaries who lived in other cities. In 1984, we started each day with congregational singing and special music, then had a devotional message by Mark Corts, pastor from Winston Salem. Our only instruments were a guitar and an accordion. It was like listening to a large choir where 80% were soloist quality. I got goosebumps from listening to it.

*   *   *   *

When we returned from furlough in 1984, I was persuaded to play on the clinic's women's softball team. I played as the designated hitter. I had always been good at athletic games, and even at forty-six years old, I could still hit the ball well. The next oldest player was thirty-two. I couldn't run worth a hoot, but I could hit runners in. I slid into second base knocking the second baseman down on top of me, tearing all the ligaments in my left foot, thus, ending my softball career. I managed to hobble around the bases to make a run but had to go to the hospital for treatment after the game.

* * * *

It seemed that every time that we went home on furlough, the church would suffer a crisis. During one of these times, the pastor was asked to leave. Rumors were flying, mud was thrown everywhere, tempers were rising and Satan had a heyday. When we left, there had been an average attendance of one hundred seventy-five to one hundred eighty on Sunday, but on return, there was forty-five on a good day. We visited with many of the people who had left the church and united with another church, including the former pastor, to let them know that we loved them and supported them. Those who were still embittered and left the church completely, we tried to convince to join some other congregation. With our own church, we tried not to be judgmental or critical, but realized what was done was done and that now we must work together to strengthen the Lord's work. Ausberto Guerra, a young pastor graduating from the seminary in a couple of months, had answered the call to be the new pastor. We had worked with him when he was a youth, and he was a fine young man. We were excited about his coming and prayed that the people would respond to him.

For our Christmas cantata, we put together a program with narration and slides that we projected onto the wall depicting the Christmas Story. We had chosen Christmas music that would verbally illustrate the pictures and the real meaning of Christmas. We called it "Come, Worship! Go, Proclaim!". Of the forty-five who were attending the church, seventeen of them sang in the choir. We prayed that this would help in the healing process for everyone.

* * * *

In February 1985, Robert and I went on a caravan to Miraflores, Sucre. We drove seven hours to San Marcos, left our car and traveled in an open cattle trailer pulled by a tractor to a ranch where we set up camp. We were supposed to make it in four hours by tractor, but we managed to make it in only fourteen hours. A wheel bearing went out on the trailer when we were out in the middle of nowhere with no spare parts on a Sunday. A cowboy passing by found an old, rusty bearing on his ranch that he lent to us. Then, the tire kept going flat, and we had to stop and pump air in it every fifteen minutes. In the end, we were patching the tire with adhesive tape. I was afraid that we would not have any tape left for bandages.

* * * *

An excerpt from letter to Mike and Dunia February 1985 ... We are in the middle of Carnival. All the social clubs rotate having parades during the four weeks preceding the actual Carnival; the parades end up one block from our house. They block off that corner and redirect traffic to the street in front of our house; the people park their cars up and down our street. We get to "enjoy?" the party without leaving our house, and it last until 4:30AM. We live a block away, but the amplified music is so loud that it hurts our ears, I can't imagine how the hundreds of people can stand to be directly in front of the dozens of huge speakers. I must say the fireworks display this past Saturday was one of the prettiest that I have every seen. It must have cost a fortune. The vibrations of the exploding fireworks set off the alarms of cars parked in front of our house....

* * * *

1985 was a difficult year. The guerrilla group M19 took over the *Palacio de Justicia** (Supreme court building) in Bogotá and assassinated half of the supreme court judges. The images of military-armored tanks climbing up the steps to counter attack the guerrillas went out on T.V. all over the world. The guerrilla group M19 later disbanded, received amnesty, and was repatriated. It later became a legitimate political party

A week later, the Volcano Ruiz erupted and sent melted snow and a raging mud slide down a mountain valley, killing an estimated 28,000 people and destroying one town completely. The magnitude of this tragedy was almost indescribable. People lost everything they had, including all or part of their families. Our Baptist missionaries responded immediately, as did many others, sending supplies, obtaining generators, providing water and necessary food and clothing. Robert and a medical team left immediately from our clinic and spent several weeks there. Doctors from all over the world responded. There were several doctors from Japan. They said that they had been helped so often in disasters similar to this that they wanted to reciprocate. They were more experienced in trauma than many of the others and were of invaluable help. A triage area was set up in front of one of the local hospitals. Robert was passing through the halls one day, going to surgery, when he spied a young man lying on a pallet put off to one side. The patient had been evaluated as beyond help and was expected to die. It was evident that he had gas gangrene; anyone who has ever smelled gas gangrene will recognize it when it is present. José A. had just been rescued that day after being trapped in the mud for four days. Robert felt that they could do something so he began debriding the gangrene and cleaning up José. He had to amputate one of his legs, but José A. did survive. (He later sent us a picture of his baptism. Years later, he became an accountant, married and had a family). Many of these people had been literally buried alive in the mud. When the doctors began debriding the areas, they found that mud had been forced through small wounds deep into underlying tissues. Many families were separated and had difficulty finding other family members. A picture of Robert debriding a man was published in the newspaper; a member of his family recognized him, and the family was reunited.

Because bodies were discovered in rivers and streams, some as far away as four hundred miles from the actual mudslide, there was a fear of an epidemic of cholera. Everyone was advised to boil all of their drinking water and take extreme precautions. There were a few cases reported, but the epidemic fortunately, did not occur. Unfortunately, years later, unrelated to this incident, there was an outbreak of cholera in the country.

* * * *

An excerpt from Christmas letter 1985: ... I know that many of you read about the violence, economic crisis, mafia and drug traffickers in Colombia. Most of it is true, but we do not feel that we are personally in any danger. However, this country needs your prayers so that it might overcome the crisis that it is currently going through.

When we arrived more than ten years ago, most of the doctors or professional people showed very little interest in the gospel. We now have a doctor's Bible study, and there are usually between twelve and fifteen doctors and their wives in attendance. Both the director and the administrator of our hospital are wonderful Colombian Christians. Since coming back from furlough, Robert has not had to do any administrative work except on a consulting basis. This has been an answer to our prayers. Robert discovered that administration was not one of his gifts. He much prefers the medical/surgical part of caring for patients.

Since October, I have been leading a group of ladies in Bible study in the home of a Colombian Air Force Commander. Sonya, the wife of the commander, made a profession of faith while in the States on special assignment with her husband. The other four ladies are wives of Air Force officers and have never read the Bible before. It is thrilling to see how they are soaking up the Bible studies. They want to have a Bible study with their husbands, and we are planning for Robert to lead this study.

We miss our family and friends but know that they support us, knowing that this is God's will for our lives at this moment. Pray for the choir, the different Bible studies, the daily time consuming activities necessary for existence, and the wisdom to keep our priorities in proper order. Pray for the crisis here in Colombia, spiritual, economic, and political ...

* * * *

An excerpt from letter to Mike and Dunia November 1986: ... There were several fire bombings last week. Four buses were bombed and fourteen people were killed, many more were injured. *Ley's* (department store that we all frequent) was burned to the ground as were several other big stores. Bombs were discovered and dismantled in *Olímpica* (large grocery store). We are all trying to keep a low profile, but working as usual.

You would not recognize the clinic. The new outpatient clinic has opened, and it is very modern. The new chapel is also lovely. They are remodeling the E.R. and building another floor above to house ten doctors' offices ...

* * * *

Traveling in a dugout canoe heading for a remote village in the jungle, we passed a good number of isolated homes and small groups of homes along the tropical riverbank. They were mostly primitive dwellings with thatched roofs and dirt floors. Some of the women were standing at the bank scrubbing their clothes on rocks in the river or standing on the outer edge of their "floating outhouse" washing their clothes and their dishes. The conditions were rather primitive, but as we had seen others even more primitive, we did not pay any attention to them until Marta, an intern from the city, going on her first mobile medical caravan and so overcome with the extreme poverty that she was seeing, exploded with a passionate question, "Why don't you do something to help these people?"

We were so stunned that we couldn't reply.

After a brief time of silence, Marta again exploded, "Why doesn't the government do something to help these people?"

We really didn't want to handle that can of worms.

A little later, Marta cried softly, "What can I do to help these people?"

She was coming around to answering her own question. When we are interested enough to get involved ourselves and not expect others to do the work, something can and will be done.

Poverty is relative. Marta had seen a lot of poverty in and around her big city and thought that she knew all about it, but the reality of seeing people living in these extreme conditions distressed and appalled her.

Over the years, many interns have gone with us on mobile medical caravans. Dorcey Manga went with us on several, at first protesting, but later enjoyed it so much that he is now working in the red zone (guerrilla controlled area) where we are unable to go and ministering to the people both physically and spiritually. Saul Christianson went with us as an intern and later when he was in practice. He came to know the Lord, and we were *padrinos** (godparents) at his wedding. Alexi, a shy, mother's boy, loved the caravan work and volunteered to go even after finishing his training. Marta, mentioned before, was shocked by the poverty and extreme conditions that people lived in within her own country. Some went reluctantly, and some under protest. Most came back with a feeling of satisfaction and wanting to help more. Some came back rejecting completely the purpose of the caravans.

* * * *

We first saw Zaida C. when she was sixteen years old. When she was twenty months old, she was badly burned and had extensive burn contractures in her right elbow drawing her right arm almost doubling it. She could not use this arm to comb her hair, brush her teeth, or anything that required straightening the arm. Doing small plastic surgical procedures and skin grafts during five different trips (in a hospital it could have been done all at once), we were able to release these contractures. She can now straighten her arm and has full use of it. She has since left her village and completed her high school education and is living a full productive life. Without the caravan she would still be living a limited lifestyle in the jungle. It is impossible to cure all the ills of Colombia with our limited means on the caravans, but we have to view each life that has been helped and changed in some way and each drop helps to fill the bucket. Zaida is one of our drops in the bucket.

*   *   *   *

In the first few years going to the jungle area in the Chocó, we would drive seven hours to Monteria to meet the Mission Aviation Fellowship Missionaries who would fly us in Cessna planes to Vigía, Antioquia where there is a grass landing strip. They would leave us there to return in one weeks time to pick us up. From Vigía, we would take dugout canoes for another three hours or more to arrive in La Loma. One trip, we returned a day early to Vigía to await the plane and discovered that the village had dug a big ditch across the landing strip. Robert stepped the available strip off to see if there was enough room for the plane to land and take off. On return trips home, we have less weight, having given out most of our medicine; therefore he estimated that there was just enough room. When the pilot arrived and was circling, Robert tried to communicate this using hand signals. They were able to land, but they too, knowing that we would be lighter, had taken on a couple of passengers. Now there was a problem with having enough room to take off. We rigged up a 2 X 6 plank of wood across the ditch and pulled the tail section across it to use as a runway for the back wheel. The pilot revved up the motor and we all prayed. The plane took off—just—clearing the trees at the end of the runway.

This runway has always been a problem. The men in the village had to clear it with machetes each time it was used. The pilot always had to circle low to look for animals or debris before he could land. On take off, the children tried to catch a ride on the tail. We asked the priest and village council to keep the children away from the plane, for we were so afraid that one of them would get hurt.

The plane trips are always interesting. One time, with all the low clouds and turbulence, we had to fly low, just skimming the jungle treetops. We could look out the window and see the tropical birds flying alongside the plane. The pilot became disoriented and couldn't find the village. He told us that we had enough fuel for five more minutes of search, and then we would have to return to home base. All of a sudden, there appeared an opening in the clouds, and in that clearing was our little village.

Another time, we were flying about 9,000 feet and suddenly, the cabin filled with smoke. It was a scary feeling for a while as we all looked to see what was on fire. On the ground, people were burning a field, and the smoke had risen and entered the plane.

Zack Deal, one of our missionaries living in Medellín, was taking a beehive with 25,000 honey bees to give to the people in the jungle. This is a very poor part of the country, and he thought that the people could sell what honey they didn't eat. The bees made more noise than the motor of the plane. We prayed that none of the bees got loose in the cabin while we were in the air. The bees, unfortunately, did not survive in the jungle. Pollinating flowers, needed by the bees, could not survive in this dense rain forest where the average rainfall is up to 400 inches a year.

One time we arrived, and the people were complaining that it had not rained for more than eight days and it was dry. It began raining the day that we arrived. Conversation is impossible when it is raining because the roofs are made of tin, and when it rains so hard, it sounds like a freight train passing through the house. The houses are all built on stilts to protect them from flooding. We were sitting on the second floor balcony watching the river rise. In twenty-four hours, the river rose more than ten feet. Folks that is a lot of rain!

Another time, we went to Napipí, and again it had not rained for several days. The people all have big fiberglass tanks to collect rainwater for drinking. Because the people had not maintained them, they were all broken and empty. They were using river water for everything. We tried to teach the people that they must boil all their water and never drink or give us anything that has not been boiled. It was extremely hot, we were tired and did not question them when they brought us glasses of beet juice. I chug-a-lugged about half of the glass before putting it down and then three wrigglers (Mosquito larvae) rose to the top of the glass. There was no telling how many I had swallowed. Everyone else had done the same thing. That night, I was very sick with vomiting and diarrhea. All that night it rained hard. You have to have a sense of humor to survive some of the events. Later, I could laugh but not at that moment. Have you ever tried to juggle an umbrella, T.P., a flashlight, and your clothes all at once, trying not to drown from the tropical rain?

There are no bathrooms there, only what we call floating outhouses (a raft, of sorts, floating on the river with four walls and sometimes a roof and a hole in the floor that you straddle). You walk a narrow, slippery, bobbing plank to get to them. When you are well, it is difficult to cross, but when you are sick and in a hurry, it is impossible. I was afraid that I would land up in the river if I tried to go that route. Neither did I want to penetrate the jungle. At night, the people just go wherever is handy. I was only interested in going to a different place each time. Robert, Dorcey and Pastor José DeMoya teased me about women being frail and not being able to take difficult conditions. It took the fellows a couple of days before it hit them. Our whole team had severe vomiting and diarrhea for eight days. We continued working because we had to wait for the plane to return to Vigía.

It was on this trip that we ate one or our most interesting meals. The cook told us that we were eating curassow (a tropical turkey-like bird). Robert, who is an avid bird watcher and knows most of the birds of Colombia, knew that it was not turkey or curassow, but didn't want to tell us what he thought it was (it could have been a buzzard). Later, he went walking with some of the village children, and they saw a bunch of feathers. Robert stopped to examine them, and the kids said that the feathers were from the bird that we had eaten for lunch. He brought back a souvenir to show us. It was a Harpy Eagle. He said, "I feel positively un-American eating eagle." It was the toughest and worst-tasting thing that I have ever tried to eat. It was very dark meat and had a strong, unpalatable flavor. We have eaten strange things before but nothing that was as bad tasting as this. Robert said that because I was already sick, anything would have tasted bad. He did not think it was *that* bad-tasting.

* * * *

The Mission Aviation Fellowship (MAF) had to leave Colombia because of increasing violence in the areas where they flew. When they left Colombia, it was difficult to get to the Chocó. The first time we went after they left, we flew commercial planes from Barranquilla to Medellín and then to Quibdó, the capital of Chocó. We spent the night in Quibdó and hired a dugout the next day to carry us to La Loma. It took eighteen hours. It started to rain hard in the afternoon, and when the lightening got bad, we pulled over to the bank and decided to rest until the weather let up some. We spread tablecloths on the floor of a schoolhouse for a community bed and everyone tried to rest. The roof and walls leaked like a sieve, but it was drier than in the boat. The jungle is hot and steamy, especially in the daytime, but when it rains, it gets very cold. We all huddled together trying to keep warm and dry. While we were on the river, the guide had a lot of trouble with the motor; the shear pin kept breaking and the transom broke off. We had to dock on the river's edge to try to repair it. We finally made it to the branch of the Bojayá River very late at night. La Loma in on this river. The river was low, and there was a lot of trash floating on top and under the surface of the water. It was pitch black, and the driver did not see a huge branch just under the water, and so we drove right up into the bend of the branches and got stuck. Robert and I were the only ones on board who knew how to swim. It was a miracle that we did not turn over. The people on board started to panic as we were in the middle of the river rocking back and forth and unable to move forward or backward. There was no one on the river as it was around 2:00 AM. The group began to scream *Socorro!** (Help!), in case there was anyone on the banks to hear, but no one was there in the thick jungle. After about an hour, an elderly man in a small canoe came poling down the river. One by one, and box by box, he carried us to the shore. Then, several of the men went back to our bigger canoe and bounced on the branch and shook the canoe until it finally came lose. We reloaded and started out again, finally arriving at La Loma around 6:00AM. The people were waiting for us on the bank and helped unload. We were fed breakfast,—green *plátano** boiled and *café con leche**—and we started setting up to hold clinics and do surgery. We worked all day and crashed from exhaustion that night.

*   *   *   *

We worked from 8:00 AM until 6:00 PM in the Chocó. As we were closing to go to the evangelistic service, a crowd arrived with a young boy who had been cut on the back of the neck by a machete. We had to suture him by candlelight. A couple of centimeters lower or a heavier blow and it could have been fatal. As we were ready to leave, another two children were brought in. They had been running and collided, leaving the front tooth of a little boy embedded in his sister's forehead. Robert extracted the tooth, cleaned it, replaced it into the little boy's mouth, and applied pressure. Three days later, it was as tight as the rest of his teeth. The small sister's head had to be sutured.

By the time we were ready to leave, we were so tired that we were ready to go to our room, eat, and go to bed. We decided that we had to at least make an appearance at the evangelistic service. The place was packed as we slipped into the back and sat on the ground thinking no one would see us in the candlelight. To our consternation, one of the neighbors had seen us pass his house and brought chairs for us to sit on, and then he joined us. He had been to the clinic that afternoon but had not planned on attending the services until he saw us arrive and knew that we must be exhausted. Unfortunately, these were the most uncomfortable chairs that you can imagine, straight up and down and hard as a rock. We had to sit in them to be polite. That night, he accepted Christ as his Savior. What might have been the story if we had not made the effort to go that night? Since then, we have always tried to attend the services at all the caravans unless we were still tied up in surgery.

*   *   *   *

We had just set up our clinics in Napipí, in the Chocó jungle area, when Segundo arrived with his sister. A thorn wound, eight days before, had resulted in a badly infected hand. Thinking that she was going to die, Segundo and his buddies had been out drinking all night mourning her imminent death. We told them to return the next morning after his sister had fasted, and we would drain the abscess. The next morning, we gave her I.V. anesthesia to start the procedure. People sometimes have weird reactions to one of these drugs, and she was one of the weirdest. First, we opened up the abscess, drained about a half-pint of pus, cleaned it out thoroughly, and dressed it. As she was coming out from the effects of the anesthesia, she began singing hauntingly, "… I …'..m d..e..a..d, A.n.d w..h..o i..s g..o..i..n..g to b..u..r..y m..e..?" Segundo, who was on the other side of the curtain, heard her and became hysterical, thinking that his sister was dead. Still inebriated, he and his buddies had spent the night drinking, celebrating the fact that we were going to take care of his sister. After getting him calmed down, he and his buddies went out again to celebrate the recovery of his sister.

We traveled back to Barranquilla on Robert's birthday and got back home around 10:30 PM. Jennifer was waiting for us and had made her dad a heart-shaped Jell-O dessert decorated with whipped topping. She had wanted to make him a cake or cookies but couldn't find all the ingredients and couldn't remember how I made brown sugar. We could not buy brown sugar, so I would mix ¼ tsp. of a liquid called *dulce quemada** (burnt sugar) with a cup of plain granulated white sugar, and voilá—like magic—you had brown sugar or a resemblance thereof.

*   *   *   *

Several months later, we again arrived in the pueblo of Napipí just before dark after traveling five hours in a dugout canoe. The people greeted us very cordially and set up our sleeping quarters. We were happy to see that it was a different location than our previous trip when the local cantina, with the only generator in the pueblo that powered the loud music, kept us awake all night. The pueblos in the jungle do not have electricity but usually have at least one generator. These are usually found in the cantinas where all the men congregate to drink beer and *aguardiente** (a type of cheap liquor) and play dominoes and loud music. We didn't realize until it got dark that the cantina had moved and was fifty feet from where we were to sleep. The first night, we couldn't rest because the music was so loud. After working hard all day in extreme heat, we needed to be able to rest at night. The people were all shouting, slapping dominoes on the tables, and drinking most of the night. Many of these men came to see us for treatment at the clinic during the day, including the owner of the bar. The second night, I asked the owner if he would turn the music down to allow us to rest. He agreed readily. When the music was still going at 10:00 PM, I ask him again nicely to turn the music down. When he agreed and still did nothing, I marched over, pointed my finger at him, and promised him if he did not turn off the music or find us a quiet place to sleep, that in the morning, we would leave the pueblo and never return. That got everyone's attention. They all jumped up to move us to the opposite end of the pueblo and set up our hammocks in an empty school room. As they left to continue with their drinking and partying, we settled down for a much needed rest, to the peace and quiet of the normal jungle sounds. The Colombian pastor, José DeMoya, and the intern were sleeping on the other side of the partition. I saw a flashlight beaming up in the rafters, and I asked the pastor if he had problems. He laughed and said, "No, I'm checking to see if the rats are gnawing on our hammock ropes." He couldn't decide which was the bigger pest, the rats running up and down the rafters chewing on everything or the people in the cantina. We all decided that the rats were the lesser of the two pests. We all went to sleep content, knowing that, at that moment, the rats were not gnawing on our hammock ropes.

*   *   *   *

Many of the pueblos along the river had the "floating bathrooms". You could often see women washing their dishes and clothes around the rim of the outhouse, and others washing and preparing the food that they would cook for the next meal. Someone else would stand on the edge and bathe, brush his or her teeth, while someone else would be inside relieving himself. They would then come to the clinics complaining of stomach and intestinal problems and not believe us when we told them how to cure their problems. Medicine was temporary. They had to change their sanitation practices. Their parents lived that way, and so did their grandparents, and they were not about to change because a group of *gringos* told them that there was a better way of doing things. TRADITION!!!

You could see drastic changes in some pueblos from one visit to the next. They were eager to learn how to help themselves. Others like Napipí were only interested in what they could get out of us. If they had to work or change their way of doing things, they weren't interested. There is so much need in all of that area, but if they are not interested in helping themselves, it is useless and fruitless to go there. So many areas go out of their way to cooperate and give you the best that they can, and many times give you better than what they themselves have; they are ready to do whatever needs to be done to improve their living conditions. It is a joy working with these people and watching them grow.

The nearest medical help was a small health center two hours away by river. For anything serious, they had to travel nine hours by river. One night, about midnight, a man was brought to us from down river who had been shot. We weren't able to do much except stop the external bleeding and start several I.V.'s trying to stablize him. We then had to transport him by canoe to the nearest hospital which was nine hours away, but he died shortly after arriving there.

The arrival of the medical caravan was a very special event. We normally stayed a week and, during that time, saw from four hundred to five hundred people. For surgery, we carried our own sterilizing equipment (in the early years we used a cold sterilizing solution that we soaked everything in, then we got smarter and used a pressure cooker—this was tricky controlling the pressure using an open wood fire). Anesthesia was local (Lidocaine) and/or very light intravenous (Valium and Ketamine). The light source was another person holding flashlights. Robert had to wear sweat bands made out of rolled up surgical gauze around his head and wrist due to the usual 90 degrees plus temperatures and 100% humidity; he often had to raise his hands above his shoulders to let the perspiration run out of his surgical gloves.

We ate whatever the people provided for us which was usually plain boiled white rice, soup, plantains, and occasionally, fish. The intense heat resulted in having to drink a lot of liquids, most often Colombian coffee or fruit juices and/or coconut water at room temperature. Because we perspired so much, we had to eat extra salt each day. They often offered us their beds to sleep in, but they were usually very hard (sometimes it was a thin sheet covering boards), and short for us and sometimes buggy. We preferred to sleep in hammocks but slept in whatever they provided. We would never have done anything to offend or hurt them. They gave the best that they had, and it came from their hearts.

*   *   *   *

The Kogi are a very handsome people and very proud. When we were in Momorongo, a young Kogi Indian boy came to see us. None of his baby teeth had fallen out when his permanent teeth came in, and he had a double row of teeth, top and bottom. He was an embarrassment to his family and the tribe. They thought that he was a freak so he was ostracized. Although Robert is a surgeon, he has often had to do general medicine and dentistry. Robert said that he could pull his baby teeth but couldn't do it all at once. He asked the boy when he wanted to do it, and he was ready right then. We anesthetized one side of his mouth and pulled all the baby teeth on that side. We told him about Jesus and how He loved the little boy so much that he sent people to help him. We told him that we had to wait until he regained the feeling on that side before we could pull the teeth on the other side. He was such a good patient and never even flinched or cried out. He was back that afternoon, smiling, and ready to have the rest of his baby teeth pulled. He left the room with his mouth full of bloody gauze and a grin from ear to ear. His family and the rest of the tribe were amazed and called it a "miracle". He was a "hero" and he was accepted back into the fold. He went back telling them about Jesus and His Love.

During a break time, we walked up a mountain trail so that Robert could see the birds in the area. I soon got tired and stopped to rest under a tree to wait for Robert and the young medical student to return. I shortly heard a voice say *Hunchaka!** Mariana, a young Kogi woman who had been in our home several months before, was standing on the trail. She invited me to her home on the mountainside where her mother had given birth to a baby five hours previously. She left one of her brothers to watch for Robert's return. I went with her inside the hut, where her mother lay on a pallet on the floor. A fire was burning in the middle of the room, as is the custom, and a pot of soup was cooking on the open fire. The baby was bundled up so tight that he couldn't move. They insisted that I had to kneel down before the fire and hold the baby. It was cold outside, but by the fire, it was very hot. They were all very cordial and offered me something to drink and eat. They took "the" tin cup off of a post and dipped it into a pot and gave me something to drink. It wasn't too bad but I couldn't drink it all and left about an inch of liquid in the cup. Mariana then gave a sip to about five snotty, dirty-faced little boys sitting around. She then put the cup on top of the post again without washing it. When Robert and Kevin arrived, she dipped the same cup into the pot and gave them each a drink. It is a miracle that none of us got sick. Before the fellows arrived, they offered me some of the soup. It was tasty, but I made the mistake of asking what it was. It was rat soup. I managed to swallow without gagging. (I remembered Vicente eating a HOT DOG in my home). Meat is very scarce in the mountain area where they live so they eat whatever is available. If they eat it, and the Lord provided it, how could I refuse to eat it? I later found out that I was highly honored by being invited to eat because they are very leery of non-Kogi people, and they never invite an outsider to enter their home and certainly, never share their meal. They were returning the hospitality that I had offered Mariana a few months before.

Robert celebrated his birthday while we were working in the village, and the missionaries made him a pineapple upside down cake over an open fire; they had no oven. It was very good. Twenty four years later, we received an e-mail from this missionary who said that she and ten Kogi Indians were celebrating the twenty-fourth birthday of Alberto, a Kogi Indian who was born on Robert's birthday while we were there, and that they were all praying for Robert. To us that was a very moving remembrance.

* * * *

In Sucre, the people made us a surgery table by burying four bamboo poles into the dirt floor, placing a split bamboo table across them, and then covering this with a woven bamboo mat. The height and width were just right for us. It was the first time that we did not have to lean over and suffer terrible backaches at the end of the day. The room had a dirt floor, thatch roof and bamboo walls. We had chickens, dogs and pigs running under the operating table. There was a hen that was accustomed to laying her eggs in the corner of the room, and every time that the door opened, she'd run to go to her corner—the one where we soaked our instruments in a sterilizing solution. We were afraid that she would contaminate everything, so we were constantly running her out. She was so persistent that we finally had to remove our solutions and let her in. She laid her egg, cackled her triumph, and left happy—until the next time. We had to learn how to be flexible in these circumstances. The bonus was that we had a fresh egg for breakfast.

* * * *

In the Llanos, during the day the people stand around waiting to be seen by the doctors, they eat *corozos** (fruit from special palm trees that have big seeds about the size of a marble). They eat the fruit and spit the seeds on the ground. At night, while everyone has their hammocks strung all around the eaves, we listen to the pigs chomping on the corozo seeds. One night, Kay R. panicked, thinking they were eating the food that we had stored on the tables. She said, "Jeni, I think the pigs are eating our food."

Jeni replied sleepily, ... "Hummm ... no, Kay."

A little later Kay said, "JENI, the pigs are eating our food."

Jeni grunted and said, "No, Kay."

The third time Kay forcefully said, "JENI, THE PIGS ARE EATING OUR FOOD!!!"

The disgruntled people in hammocks outside the house all hollered, "No, Kay, they are eating corozo seeds, go-o-o to sleep!"

A cool wind came up during the night, and everyone and everything began to get cold. We didn't have blankets, and sleeping in hammocks allows the cold to penetrate your whole body. The pigs all gathered against the wall next to Robert's hammock. They piled up, one on top of the other, to keep warm. Ever so often, they changed places, the one on the bottom going to the top and vice-versa. They kept grunting and making so much noise that he lifted his mosquito net, reached out, and swatted the rump of the one closest to him to get them to move. Instead, he startled them, and they panicked. They ran under his mosquito net before he could let it drop, and in their panic, they literally ripped his netting to shreds trying to get out.

*   *   *   *

During the dry season, we are able to drive in to the Llanos (Eastern Plains of Colombia). There are no roads, but we have guides who lead us through open fields and dirt trails. Once, we took two pickup trucks that had been converted into station wagons. Robert drove one, and Ross Thompson drove the other. We had a medical student from the States riding with us, plus a couple of local people who acted as guides. With Ross, rode his son, Charles, and a national pastor. The cars kicked up so much dust that the second car had to drive a good distance behind the first car, following the dust cloud. We kept in touch using walkie-talkies. Our code names were Moses and Pharaoh, not very original, but very appropriate. We were Moses, and Ross was Pharaoh. The verbose pastor was a person who did not spend much time in silence. Ross was a person who liked his silence. At one point, we looked in the rear view mirror, and we caught a glimpse of the other car a few meters behind us. We wondered why they were traveling in the middle of all that thick dust until we saw Ross, grinning from ear to ear, and the pastor with his handkerchief covering his mouth. Ross had found a solution to his problem. Sometimes our sense of humor finds weird outlets.

* * * *

The first four years that we were in Colombia we had an average of four days out of the week that we had from three to thirteen visitors staying with us. Our home was nicknamed the "Edwards Hilton." This hospitality continued for the thirty years that we stayed in Colombia. The majority were very enjoyable, but some were pains in the neck. I remember one couple from Sucre who came for medical attention in Barranquilla and stayed several weeks with us. They were accustomed to getting up at 4:30 every morning and wanting their *tinto** (small demitasse of black coffee). I do not do mornings well; but I tried to be polite, and prepared their *tinto*. They were very pushy and were always looking for handouts. I later overheard the lady talking on the phone, telling someone that "no, they could not stay with their family; they needed to stay with the Doctor." When I found out that they had family living in Barranquilla and could just as easily have stayed with them, I really lost my cool and refused to let them stay with us again. In fact, I told the Pastor of their church that from here on, whenever anyone came to the city for treatment, they had to find another place to stay. My "hotel" had closed. Nevertheless, we had so many enjoyable visitors; they made up for the few who took adantage of us.

Pastor Tulio always stayed with us when he came to Barranquilla. He was a joy to have. One time, he put his extra pair of trousers on the bed next to the window. The pants contained all the money that he had brought with him for the trip's expenses. Someone climbed the outside gate and used a wire to snatch Tulio's trousers through the window. We could not leave anything of value near a window. Once, I caught someone trying to steal a sheet off of the bed using a wire snatch. When we had company we had to leave the window open for ventilation; when no one was there, we closed and locked them.

* * * *

The world is truly a small place. We directed the English-speaking Chapel for the first eight years we were in Colombia. A single young man from Kentucky, George Morgan, attended and became part of our extended family. His grandparents, who lived in the Rio Grande Valley of Texas, were patients of my father-in-law, who was a family practice doctor there. Robert remembered George's mother, Josie. Since that time, we have received cards from Josie every birthday and holiday.

In the summer of 1981, Deedee Winfield came as a volunteer. We had been members of the same Sunday School class with Deedee and her husband when Robert was in the Air Force in San Angelo, Texas back in 1962.

Tom Smoke was a pilot for the Wyclliff Bible Translators. He spent the night at our house before flying us up into the Sierra Nevada mountains to do a mobile medical clinic with the Kogi Indians. He asked about a painting on our wall that Robert had painted several years before. It was a scene of the Llanos, the Eastern Plains of Colombia. He asked if we had ever been there. We said yes, that Robert had painted the picture using a photo found in the National Geographic magazine in the '70's. Tom laughed and told us if we looked in the lower right-hand corner we might see his plane. He happened to have flown the photographer around Colombia for that article, and he remembered him taking that particular picture. His plane was just out of the camera range.

* * * *

This was the time of Pablo Escobar, the drug lord's rise and fall. I read the book *KILLING PABLO* by Mark Bowden and recognized several incidences that we had lived through. It was not an easy time to live in Colombia. I had been given a ham radio to be able to easily communicate with family and friends back in the States, and I was in the process of getting my ham radio license when all the violence escalated. The guerrillas, the drug lords, the army and others were monitoring radio messages, cell phones, as well as land phones. I took down my antenna, and stopped the license process at once, and never used the radio again.

Some of the drug cartel were being extradited to the United States. All the North Americans living in Colombia were told to keep a low profile because retaliation against U.S. citizens was a possibility. Robert's method of keeping a low profile was to take a nap. We didn't want to be foolhardy, nor did we want to be ruled by fear. God gave us a peace, knowing that where He wanted us to be was the safest place to be. That does not guarantee that nothing will happen, but He will sustain you through all things.

* * * *

Rosalba was a thirty-seven-year-old mother/grandmother dying with cancer. She had two children, ages fourteen and twenty-one, and a three-year-old granddaughter. Rosalba was lying on a dirty pallet on the cement floor of an airless shack. She was moaning, crying, and screaming constantly when we arrived to visit with her. She was in the last stages of cancer and was only taking a low dosage Tylenol for the pain. LuzMery, from our group, knelt down on the pallet with her and began stroking her hand and talking soothingly to her. LuzMery prayed with her and told Rosalba that God loved her and wanted to give her peace and comfort. The longer LuzMery talked, the calmer Rosalba became until she asked Jesus to come into her heart as her Lord and Savior. In spite of her physical pain, her face radiated with an inner peace. She lost her fear of dying and said that she was ready to meet her Lord. We took her to the clinic to see Robert to get a stronger pain reliever, but Rosalba went to be with the Lord two days later. Her friends mourned but declared how good and merciful the Lord was, He had allowed her to live long enough to know and accept Him personally, and now she was with Him in Heaven in all His Glory.

* * * *

Excerpt to a friend: ... Robert and I just returned from a mobile medical trip to Sucre. We had traveled for seven hours on mostly paved roads. Since it was the dry season, we were able to drive, using four-wheel-drive vehicles, on dirt levies for another seven hours to reach a small community called Miraflores. In the rainy season, we travel by dugout canoe for seven to nine hours more to reach the same place because the levies are all under water. It was very hot, several days of 105°F. We treated more than six hundred patients and did around sixty surgeries in only five working days. Our sleeping quarters had a dirt floor, bamboo/mud walls, and a thatched roof. They insisted that Robert and I sleep in a bed (three-quarter size) that was very firm. We had no problem with the "unfriendlies" (leftist guerrillas) although we did attend some of them in the clinic. A couple of times, Robert unthinkingly asked someone what work that they did, in hopes of finding out why they were having pain. One fellow looked at Robert, and then looked at me, and I quickly told Robert to rephrase the question. The guy did not answer at first, but when we asked if he rode horseback a great deal or lifted heavy objects, he did answer in general terms. You don't ask people in this area what they do, or they might tell you, and you really don't want to know. This was the first time that we were able to go to this community in one and a half years because of the guerrilla activity.

* * * *

A Colombian dentist went with us to Miraflores to pull teeth. He was eager to help and do whatever he could to help the people. He quickly learned that each area of the country had its own colloquialisms. A patient, who had just had surgery, asked him how long the doctor meant for her to "stay on a diet." Trying to be helpful, the dentist emphatically said, if the doctor told her to stay on a diet, it meant for life. When we explained to him that in this area the idiom "stay on a diet" meant to refrain from sexual relations, the dentist was horrified. He thought he had ruined the patient's life.

* * * *

I don't know if the following story is true or not, but knowing Ruffo who told it to us, it could well be true. "Everyone wanted to be invited to the most prestigious society wedding of the year in Barranquilla. To attend, all the men were required to wear tuxedos. Ruffo was excited to get an invitation, and he did own a tux. But wait,—he had lent it to his neighbor. He ran to the neighbor's house to retrieve his tux, but unfortunately he found that his neighbor had died the night before. As he passed by the coffin in their home, tears ran down his cheeks. His neighbor was being buried in Ruffo's tux."

* * * *

When we were in the jungle area of the Chocó, our diet was somewhat limited. It is so wet that many foods will not grow. Cattle is non-existent as there is no grass, and the only things that will grow in abundance are plantains. Some people have small gardens in pots that they grow on their roof, or on a shelf built on stilts up off the ground. They do have ducks, chickens, plenty of eggs, and fish when they can be caught. They eat a lot of canned meat such as tuna and sardines. But the one thing that you can always count on at every meal is plantain. Plantains are very good and there are many ways to prepare them. However, boiled green plantains have <u>no</u> taste; it is what I imagine eating an art gum eraser would taste like. It plugs you up, and it also produces a lot of gas. You never want to walk behind a horse that has eaten a lot of plantains (that is a voice of experience). For breakfast, our medical team would each be served a bowl of boiled green plantains. Pastor José DeMoya notoriously arrived late for breakfast. One morning, we all piled our plantains on his plate. When he sat down, he looked at his plate, then looked up at us. Bless his heart, he ate every bite and we all felt guilty.

Dominga, the mother of Elena, wanted to send a treat to her daughter who had to stay behind and work in Barranquilla. Dominga put a couple of plastic bags filled with *chontodura** in the side pocket of our tote bags. When we got home, we told Elena that we would have to charge her for the extra passengers that had hitched a ride from the jungle. The bags were filled with roaches that had evidently hidden inside the husk of the *chontodura*.

* * * *

When we first arrived in Colombia, we had a lot to learn about the culture. Sometimes, when you asked someone what their occupation was, they would proudly reply *Contrabandista*.* We quickly learned not to show any judgmental attitude. These people were proud of having a lucrative job and being able to support their families. To them, it was an honorable profession; at this time, they were not dealing in drugs. The drug-trafficking became a problem in the years to come, and there was a big difference between a *contrabandista* and the "drug cartel." We learned not to look at situations from our American standpoint, but tried to see from their viewpoint. For example, to the Colombia Christian, drinking is a sin, and to get drunk is unpardonable, but to work in a liquor factory is an honorable employment.

* * * *

We tried not to make a big deal out of every controversy that we encountered so that we would have more influence when we did find something that we could not keep quiet about. Machismo is prevalent in Colombia, and one of its by-products is infidelity in marriage. The women cry and lament about their husbands' unfaithfulness. In the next breath, they say that it is only natural for a man to be unfaithful, hence, they must resign themselves to it. I told them that they were at fault by teaching their children that it was acceptable. Their sons were taught that this was their "right", and their daughters were taught to submit to this indignity. Robert came across the same situation with a group of his colleagues. They were discussing how terrible it was for a woman to be unfaithful. This would destroy the marriage, however, the husband was only doing what was natural and therefore, it did not affect his marriage or his feelings for his wife and family. In the middle of this discussion they turned to Robert and asked him for his opinion. He was very diplomatic. He first quietly inquired where they had gotten married. When they all answered "in church", he asked them if they had taken vows. They responded "yes." Robert asked if they had made their vows before "the priest, God, their wife and family." When they again replied "yes," he questioned if their word meant anything. There was a brief silence, and then they hung their heads and nothing more was said.

* * * *

When we arrived Catholicism was a state religion. The Colombians stated that about 97% of them were Catholic, but only about 10% were practicing Catholic. We did not go to Colombia to make everyone a Baptist, but to share Jesus and His Saving Grace and teach them how to have a personal relationship with Him. We feel that when we get to Heaven, we will rejoice with many Christian brethren of other denominations. We met and worked alongside many dedicated Christians of other faiths. God looks at the inner man, not just his label. We once heard Sam Canata, a beloved missionary who worked for many years in Africa, say, "I have spoken in many ultra conservative churches in the States, and I have spoken in the other kind. I have not seen any difference in either of their lifestyles."

* * * *

.The economic situation here keeps getting worse. It breaks your heart seeing so many people who don't have enough to eat. A couple of our missions have begun collecting food baskets. When they have a cup of rice left over, a few beans, or a little oil they bring it to the church so that they can help someone who is desperate. They know that at any time they could be the one asking for the basket, so they are trying to help one another. This is only a temporary help, and at the moment, we haven't found a more permanent solution. People need jobs, but there are none, instead, people are being laid off. The official unemployment rate is 22%, but in many of our neighborhoods where we work, it is 90%.

* * * *

An excerpt from letter to Louise McFerrin:... Prayer and patience bring many blessings. Benigno, the husband of one of our believers, has resisted the gospel for several years. His wife, Mabel and their two older children have made professions of faith and have been baptized. They have prayed for Benigno and tried to be a loving family without nagging. Benigno has recently come to know Jesus as his personal savior and wants to be baptized. Before, he did not see the need to legalize his union, but now, he wants to be legally wedded to Mabel at the same time of his baptism. Mabel and the children were crying with joy at the change that they have seen in their husband and father. We give God the honor and glory and thank Him for giving the family patience and love.

There are many, many more individuals who have been affected by the Gospel. Missions is all about people as individuals. Seeing the changed lives and the excitement as they grow, and being able to encourage them in their pilgrimage with the Lord is worth it all.

The letter ended with these prayer requests:

*Pray for the people of Colombia who are suffering circumstances that are hard for outsiders to even imagine. Their sons, husbands and fathers are being murdered or kidnapped, and the rest of the family have to flee for their lives. They are poorly educated and often have to resort to crime and prostitution in order to survive.

*Pray for the safety of the missionaries

*Pray for the safety of the nationals.

*Pray that leaders will be trained for all the new works.

*Pray for all the new Christians and their growth in their new faith.

* * * *

During a midweek Bible study, a man repairing a sewing machine in the house where we were holding the study became curious. He had accepted the Lord thirty years before; he had been rejected by evangelical groups for failure to legalize his marriage, even though his situation was almost impossible to correct. Because of this, he had never been baptized. The group invited him to participate in the Bible study. One woman who knew his situation said to him, "Don't worry, people here love you and will take care of you." He joined the group for the study and promised to continue coming each week.

* * * *

Aida, our long time home helper was a God-send. She worked nineteen years for us. When she came to us, she had just dropped out of school so that she could help her family economically. She knew nothing about cooking or cleaning a home other than her own humble house; the ways of gringos were frightening to her. Aida was eager to learn, and she soon became part of our family. I couldn't have managed without her. She was always there when I needed her, and I often used her as a sounding board when I was preparing a Bible study, a presentation, or a class. She would do most anything, except confront a rat. We had a lot of rats that came into our home, and we had to hunt them down and kill them. One day, she came inside screaming *Socorro!** Robert and I ran outside and sure enough the dog held a rat in her mouth that she had killed in Aida's room. When we ran out to the patio, Aida slammed the door and shut herself inside. The door automatically locked, and Robert and I did not have a key to get back in. Aida began screaming again, and through the window, we saw her standing on the dining table. A live rat was inside with her and we could not get inside to help her until she got down and opened the door. There had been an epidemic of leptospirosis, and at least twelve people had died with this disease. One of the diseases' carriers is rats and their excretions. Our dog had been vaccinated for it, but none of the humans in our house had been. The deaths had been human.

* * * *

I had a hard time saying "no." Because of this, I often found myself so busy that I seemed to be running round in circles. I recently reread a letter that I wrote to my family, and upon seeing all the activities that I was involved in at that time, I wonder how I ever got anything done. I wrote that at that time I was busy preparing the weekly Wednesday night Bible studies that I presented in a poor neighborhood, preparing the programs for the weekly WMU at the church, preparing and teaching the monthly cooking classes held in my home, preparing and teaching the Sunday School lessons each week, promoting the Stewardship programs in all the churches of the association, speaking at a number of churches, and presenting programs to various organizations in the city. All of these had to be prepared in Spanish which took me a lot more time, thought, study, and prayer. This was all in addition to the everyday needs of my family and the running of the household: such as shopping, cooking, and paying bills.

If it had not been for the support and help of Aida, I would not have had the time to do all of those things. She took over the cleaning of the house, the cooking, and answering the phone and the door. We averaged four nights a week with visitors. We loved having people stay with us and "The Edwards Hilton" was kept occupied most of the time. Jim and Marilyn Oliver were staying with us when they came to Barranquilla to get their physical exams. One of the exams that Jim was to have was a colonoscopy. The preparation for this exam is drinking a gallon of prepared pink liquid that cleanses the intestines. Jim, knowing that Robert was also scheduled to have this test, had bought two gallons of the pink liquid. Robert, knowing that Jim was scheduled also bought two gallons; therefore we had an abundance of pink liquid in the refrigerator. A couple of days later, after Jim and Marilyn had left, Karl Wallace came to town for a meeting. He stayed with us at least once a month when he came for clinic board meetings. He is like family also, so he comes in and makes himself at home. He came out of his room with this funny look on his face, holding up his half empty glass asked, "What in the world is in this "pink lemonade?!?" I burst out laughing and asked him how much of it that he had drunk; our plumbing could not take another all-night assault.

Every day, we had an average of ten beggars coming to the house asking for food, clothing, and/or money. I had a policy of not giving money, but always had food, and sometimes clothing. Two of the most memorable beggars were Jonny and Bautista. For about four years Jonny, a young man in his early 20's, would ring our doorbell two or three times a day asking for something. He said that his mother had left him in the care of an uncle when she moved to the U.S. His uncle would get drunk and abuse Jonny and kick him out on the street. Robert took pity on Jonny and tried to help him. He gave Jonny a physical exam and discovered that he had diabetes. Robert talked with the social worker at the clinic, Amparo, and they arranged for the clinic to provide Jonny with syringes and insulin. Amparo discovered that Jonny was selling the syringes, therefore the clinic stopped aiding him. When Jonny's foot became badly infected, Robert put him into the clinic and tried to treat his infection, but Jonny would not cooperate. Robert had to discharge him from the clinic. The last straw was when Robert discovered how Jonny was verbally abusing Aida. Robert told Jonny to never come back again. Several months later, we heard that Jonny had died in the government hospital. Everyone felt terrible, thinking that perhaps we had hastened his death. Robert and Amparo arranged to take care of his funeral. Jonny's mother and family all appeared and we learned the full extent of Jonny's lies. His mother had continually sent him money and the family had tried to help. Jonny was his own worst enemy and plunged to his own destruction.

Bautista had a wife and several children. He always had a sad story and Robert tried to help him. Over the years, Robert found him several jobs, and paid all the employment fees and physical exams required for Bautista to be employed. Each time Bautista would not show up, or would find some reason (that was never his fault) to quit. He became such a pest that the security guards at the clinic wouldn't allow him to enter, so he would camp out at our front door waiting for Robert to come home. The final straw, for me, was when Bautista wrote me a letter stating that his children were not attending school because I had not bought them shoes. I asked the Lord to give me strength not to throttle this man. I sat Bautista down and sternly told him, "I am not the parent of your children. You are! They are your responsibility. If you would spend as much time working at some of the jobs we have provided for you, as you have in trying to wheedle money out of us, you would be able to provide for your family."

* * * *

Other interesting visitors were Wade and Barbara Akins. They came to lead a conference on Pioneer Evangelism, a program for starting new churches using lay people. Wade had written the book and taught its principles all over the world. They spent all their time traveling and staying in different places. I always asked our guest what they preferred to eat for breakfast. I had just made two gallons of granola the day that they arrived. I don't enjoy cooking breakfast, but will cook the typical breakfast foods if our company wants it; but am happy when they want to eat the granola. When Wade heard that I had granola he was overjoyed. He ate three bowls of it before we left for the camp the next morning. When we got back home late at night, he ate another three bowlfuls, (this after eating supper at camp). Before they left, I had to make another big batch. He said that everyone wants to fix big meals for them which they appreciate, but since they are traveling all the time, they get a little plugged up. After eating all that granola he had no more problem.

* * * *

In all the churches in which I have been a member in the States, I have never known any of them to discipline any of its members. I witnessed one of our Colombian churches discipline two people and they were in the process of disciplining a third. This latter was a young man who was like a son to us. We had watched him grow up, and he had spent a lot of time in our home. We were excited to see him develop musically. He had a very good voice and was the unofficial music leader of the church. He was the son of one of the Baptist leaders, but also the product of a broken home. This affected him when he was younger. Pedro had been dating a girl for about a year, and they had talked about getting married some day in the future. She was now about three months pregnant so they decided to get married right away. Pedro had been a Sunday School teacher for the intermediate kids, head of the young people at the church, and held many other leadership positions. The pastor called several of us into his office to discuss the situation. Part of this group thought that the couple should not be wedded in the church and that all the church should not be invited. Others wanted to publicly discipline them. We had a very conservative church, and sometimes, it was very legalistic and strict. I sought a more loving, caring solution to the situation. I thought that we should ask Pedro to resign from his leadership positions (he had damaged his witness), but allow him to explain that it was for personal reasons; that the church should not brand this couple with a scarlet A. Everyone knew that she was pregnant, or soon would. To publicly embarrass them and kick them out of the church at a time when they desperately needed the love and support of the church was a bigger sin. I ask when did discipline stop and crucifixion begin. They finally accepted this solution. The couple were married in the church, and Robert and I were godparents. Robert also sang, and I played the piano. We all sin, but the most important thing is it how we respond to our sins. This young couple were made stronger by their response, and we love them for how they handled the whole situation.

*   *   *   *

We had been back in Colombia about a week from our furlough when one of our missionaries in the interior of the country was kidnapped at gunpoint. He was released after a couple of hours with a warning to get out of the country, which he and his family did. After consulting with the embassy and several experts on terrorist activities and members of our mission, it was decided that this was not a threat so much to the missionary community as it was to the fact that we were Americans. Things calmed down, but we continue to pray that we will know how to react wisely at all times and also know when not to react. The safety of our mission family is always a concern for prayer. We do not want to put ourselves in danger, nor do we want to put others in danger by our presence.

We spent a lot of time in prayer and consultation before we decided to continue on a mobile medical caravan. We did go, but we called a group of nurses from the States who had planned to go with us and told them not to come. It turned out to be a quiet trip of the usual long hours by four-wheel-drive vehicle followed by long hours in a dugout canoe.

It had not rained for ten days, and the creek was very low. They had to pole us through the shallow parts of the creek because it wasn't deep enough to use the motor. Even with the difficulty of transportation, we attended more than five hundred patients and did forty-nine surgeries. People traveled either by dugout, horseback or on foot. If they walked, they arrived with mud up to their knees and had to bathe in the creek before seeing one of the doctors. The church at Miraflores is really growing. They now have four missions. Due to security reasons, we were unable to have services in the church at night. However, on Sunday morning, the building was packed, and people were standing four and five deep at all the doors and windows. The church has had a big influence on the community. When we first started going there in 1981, the people were selling their eleven-year-old daughters into marriage. This practice has stopped. The general health of the community has also improved. Also of use was the training of health care promoters in the area to take care of primary health needs in our absence.

* * * *

In reading a lot of the letters that I wrote home over the years there were several items that were always on the prayer list:
*Pray for the different Bible Studies that we are leading.
*Pray for the daily time-consuming activities necessary for existence and the wisdom to keep our priorities in proper order.
*Pray for the crisis in Colombia, spiritual, economic, and political.

* * * *

In the middle of the night in the Chocó, someone came in off the river, and our host family lit candles and fed him. The walls in the rooms where we were sleeping did not go all the way to the roof. By the candle light, we could see a cat creeping down one of the crossbeams. A huge rat was walking toward him on the other crossbeam. As they met in the middle, the cat swiped at the rat, and it came flying down towards us. Robert was ready when it hit the top of our mosquito net. He hit his fist upward and sent the rat flying again, this time over the wall into the adjacent room where Zack was sleeping. Zack was such a sound sleeper that he never knew what happened. Both the cat and the rat lived to have other adventures. Robert and I tried to cover our laughter so as not to disturb our host and his guest.

* * * *

Zack and Barbara Deal were staying with us while Barbara had surgery at our hospital. They had spent thirty years in Colombia so we did not think to warn them about the *aguacera** when they left our house to go to the hospital. Zack had heard of this phenomenon, but had never experienced it. Barranquilla did not have an underground storm sewer system. There were certain streets that were planned as dry *arroyos** carrying the rain water to empty it into the river. These streets become raging torrents during a heavy rain. Most people who lived in the city knew that it was dangerous to cross one of these streets, and everyone stayed put during a rain storm. Within fifteen minutes after the rain stopped, the water would be down, and people could cross the street safely. Zack was about halfway to the hospital traveling down one of these streets designated as an *arroyo*, when the water started coming toward him rapidly. He thought that he could turn at the next corner to avoid the water, but it rose so rapidly that it stalled his car and started pushing it backwards toward the river. People on the sidewalk started screaming at them and made a human chain to help them get out of their car and reach the safety of the sidewalk. Barbara made it with their help, but Zack wanted to try to save the car. Fortunately, it was pushed up over the curb, and the back wheel got caught in a deep hole and was secured there. The tail pipe was bent, and there was so much trash underneath that someone had to saw the pipe off and clean the debris. This had a happy ending; just a week prior, a car was caught in this same spot, and it had a tragic ending when two men drowned.

* * * *

Carmen, a young paraplegic woman, lived in Sabanalarga, a city that was a forty-five-minute drive from Barranquilla. Carmen had been injured in an accident when she was a teenager. She supported herself by teaching children from her bed in her living room. We often made house visits to treat her, and she wanted to do something for us in appreciation. Our children had to read *Don Quixote* in the old Castilian Spanish. Imagine having to read Chaucer in old

English when English was not your first language. Carmen translated the book into modern-day Spanish to make it easier for our children to understand.

*   *   *   *

In the fall of 1985 we were expecting eight people to travel to the Chocó on a mobile medical trip; only four of us actually went: Robert, myself, José DeMoya and Sergio, an intern from our hospital. The week before, a band of one hundred guerillas attacked Zaiza where our plane lands to refuel. In other areas near by, there had been increased fighting causing the other team members decision not to go. When we landed in Zaiza, the people informed us that the army had cleared out the area. There had been a little excitement, and everyone had run for cover, but only two soldiers were killed. Since we were only four people plus the pilot, we decided to take only one plane. We had to lighten our load by getting rid of fifteen extra pounds of cargo. The MAF (Mission Aviation Fellowship) pilots were very strict with their weight limits, and they weighed each of us as well as each piece of cargo. We were packed like sardines into that Cessna. As usual, after we landed in Vigía we took a dugout canoe to La Loma. The poor intern had never been to the Chocó before, but he had gone to the Guajira with me on a previous trip. We had never seen the Choco so dry. It had not rained for two weeks, and this is unusual for this area. The river was only about two feet deep in many places, and the canoe had a hard time passing through. When we finally arrived at the village, the people were so appreciative. They gave Robert and me their best bed which consisted of 2 X 4's covered with sheets. One night, upon retiring, we found an egg that a hen had laid in our bed.

*   *   *   *

The intern program at our Hospital had an important influence on the lives of the young doctors passing through it. Part of the program obligations was to go on mobile medical trips when available. Very few of these young people were Christians and they only went because it was required. It had a tremendous impact on several of their lives. Many of them went through culture shock seeing all the poverty in their own country. God cares for all people, He uses people who care to help bring about change and help the needy. Several of these young doctors now have a desire to treat the physical conditions of these people, but also understand the importance of treating their spiritual condition. Several of them now attend Bible study to enrich their own spiritual life.

* * * *

While Robert was helping out at the Volcano eruption in Armero, Joan Caperton and I took a group of four doctors to the N. E. part of Colombia on a medical caravan to work with the *Wayu** Indians. One of the doctors, Dr. Jay, was from the States and had just finished his residency in internal medicine. I translated his English into Spanish, and another translator interpreted my Spanish into *Wayunike*, the language of the Indians. It was a three-ring circus. Dr. Jay learned he had to depend on his own eyes, ears, smell and touch to make a diagnosis instead of using modern lab tests and x-rays. Dr. Jay was very concerned about one of the patients. He insisted that we take her into the nearest town for x-rays and blood work. He even gave money to pay for the tests. Early in the morning, one of our helpers took the patient into Riohacha, the nearest city, trying to get the work done. She returned late that night with the patient reporting that the lab didn't have the chemicals needed to do the blood gases, nor did the x-ray department have film available for their machines, so the trip was in vain. Dr. Jay wanted me to convey simple preventative instructions to the Indian mothers bringing in children with skin disorders; the children should use shoes and clothes, and stay out of the sun and dirt. It was culture shock for him when I told him that their homes have thatched roofs with dirt floors, and their only furniture was hammocks: the children do not wear clothes (much less shoes) until they are six or seven years old, and then only a loin cloth

* * * *

Because of the heat and humidity, I can't seem to get myself organized to do anything. I go out in the mornings to buy food and do errands; I get home wringing wet, exhausted, and have to spend an hour sleeping it off after lunch.

* * * *

Evet, the sister of Mabel, lived in a *barrio** close by and loved coming to the Bible Study that I was leading in Mabel's home. One day, she was attacked in route to the study by a gang and she called the police. Evet was afraid to travel that route because she was afraid that the gang would seek revenge. Mabel agreed to lead a Bible study in Evet's home. Now we have two studies going, and more people can attend.

*   *   *   *

An excerpt from letter to Vicky Brasington March 1986 ... We just returned from a medical caravan to San Marcos, Sucre, and I believe it was one of the best that we have ever had. The church participated more and had everything ready for us to begin work. We held a dedication of their new church building. The first day, we saw one hundred general medical patients and did nine surgeries; then I lost count. Robert and Juan Carlos, one of the interns at the clinic, were the only doctors. We did a total of forty-five surgeries during the five days of work. Bob Caperton went with us and was able to drill a water well; now they have a good source of fresh water. Bob is an amazing person. Using a hand winch, he hand cranked our jeep across a stream after the jeep got stuck in the mud.

One night Juan Carlos became very upset listening to the cattle out in the pen. He thought that they must be very sick with all the bawling that they were doing. The next morning, we showed him the dozen new calves that had been born during the night. The cows had solved their own problem.

Every night, we had a service with three hundred people in attendance. Neyla, a young Barranquilla woman who went with us to help, accepted the Lord and has begun attending one of the churches here in Barranquilla. Juan Carlos gave a moving testimony the last night we were there. He wants to know more about the Gospel that motivates people to give to others and care for them without looking for, or expecting, material compensation.

*   *   *   *

An excerpt from letter to kids March 1986 ... Today was the second of four classes that I will teach on cooking desserts. There are thirteen ladies from different churches attending the class. The purpose for them is threefold: to help in the churches, to help the social ministries of the association, and to earn extra money for their families by selling baked goods. Today they brought samples of what they had learned to cook last week. Some, I believe will <u>never</u> be expert cookie makers. Last week, I taught them how to make brownies and lemon bars. Some items were not recognizable. I could tell some of them how to improve their cooking, I really didn't know what to say to others without hurting their feelings.

Julia made lemon bars using chocolate, cinnamon, and raisins. I asked her if her family liked it, and she said, "Oh yes." I then told her that she was free to change any of the recipes to her liking, but not to proclaim them as my recipes.

Yesterday was election day and it was chaotic. There was no violence that we noticed, but masses of people were everywhere. There was no public transportation, and people had difficulty getting to and from the voting locations. ELN, one of the guerilla groups, blew up a light tower, and the people were afraid that violence would erupt in the polling stations. The entire coast has been on rationed electricity for a week, and the lights are off for nine hours at a time. Yesterday and today, the water has been off. Fortunately, where we live, there is a big underground water storage tank; but we can't get it when we don't have power to pump it out. Thank goodness, I have a gas stove. Some of the missionaries who have electric stoves have had to cook their meals here. Other than the inconvenience of not having lights and only occasional water, things have been rather quite around here.

* * * *

An excerpt from letter to Charles March 1986 ... I haven't had a chance to check on ham radio operators. Your Dad saw an antenna in the next block, but you can't just knock on the door and ask if you can use their radio. You get a little uptight not knowing if people are mafioso, drug dealers or guerrillas. We have had several incidences in our neighborhood recently where the army raided homes that had stores of guns, ammunition, communication systems, radios of all types and the usual cocaine and marijuana. I had given Bob Caperton my ham radio, but it got too risky for him in the Guajira, so he returned it to me. I now have it under wraps in the back of the closet.

* * * *

Hyacinths are beautiful, blooming and floating on the water, until you have to go through them in a dugout with a small motor. They wrap around the blades of the motor, and you have to frequently stop and clean the blades. We always take a roll of wire to repair the shear pin which is certain to break at least once. As we sit trapped in the middle of a patch of hyacinths waiting for the repairs, we are surrounded by the aroma of rotting plants. It smells like raw sewage. Everyone wants to get away as rapidly as possible from the smell and the cloud of mosquitos that bombard us. A Colombian once asked me, "What is the name of the perfume that all North Americans use?" Confused at first, it finally dawned on me what he meant. I grinned and said that the perfume was called "eau de OFF."

* * * *

Jeni was traveling with a team to Sucre with Reynaldo, the son of a ranch owner, when they got lost in the middle of the swamp. Reynaldo refused to admit that they were lost, but when they finally saw a light on the water in the distance, they ask directions from a fisherman. They finally arrived at the ranch at 2:00 AM. Reynaldo's girlfriend had accompanied them as the cook. When they arrived, she wanted to know where she was to sleep; Jeni volunteered to share her sleeping quarters with her. Everyone teased Jeni about messing up Reynaldo's love life.

* * * *

On a caravan to the Llanos, on the Eastern Plains, Jeni and Kay R. were bathing in a river that had "piranhas and crocodiles". They kept their eyes on a large crocodile lying on the bank across from them as they hurriedly bathed. As they started to dry off, they noticed a humongous crocodile just four feet from them as he opened his eyes and his mouth. They grabbed their clothes and ran. (In that area there are no crocodiles. They were caimans which look like crocodiles and can be just as scary and dangerous. To Jeni and Kay they will always be crocodiles).

* * * *

In the tropical heat of the afternoon, Andrés was eating ice cream that was dripping down the front of his ragged, dirty shirt. As he walked past the home of Jimmy, he stopped to talk. Jimmy talked to him about Christ, and after a while, he asks Andrés if he would like to accept Christ as his Savior.

Andrés said, "Yeah."

Jimmy said, "Let's pray and ask Him into your heart."

Andrés, horrified said, "Like this," indicating his filth.

Jimmy explained that Christ takes us as we are, filth and all, and makes us clean.

* * * *

Sometimes we are overwhelmed with the needs of the people. We want to give them what they need and give it to them now. If we give them food or money today, they will have the same need tomorrow. We try to teach them how to help themselves so that they can eventually supply their own needs. Education is one of the ways to help them break the chain of poverty. We do not want to patronize them; we want them to keep their dignity. We provide classes to teach people how to make and sell various items such as underwear and children's clothing. They are proud when they are able to help themselves. A volunteer group from the States worked a week with Sandra, a young mother of three. Sandra lived in a one-room shack with a dirt floor, tin roof, no running water or sewage. She did not have the money to send her children to school or buy any extras; but she had such a sweet, giving spirit that the people fell in love with her. It was hard for the group to understand when we ask them not to give her money directly. We said: "Let her have the joy of giving of her time and service. She doesn't have much to give, but what she has given has been from her heart." We suggested that they might give a more lasting gift, i.e. scholarship money, so that her children could to go to school.

* * * *

Most of our medical caravans were hard work, but we left with a feeling of joy and accomplishment. There were a few times when we were heartbroken. One such time was in Sucre when a mother brought her twelve-year-old son to us complaining of belly pain. We diagnosed appendicitis and said she must take him to the nearest hospital right away (which was seven hours by dugout). We did not have the equipment or anesthesia needed for such surgery. We offered to pay for his transportation and care, and after four days, we finally convinced her to take him to the city. But it was too late. He died on the way.

* * * *

We were impressed with the people in the pueblo of Caño Chiquito in the Llanos and the leader of the church, Fraulein. There are no roads, and the only transportation is walking or on horseback. When the church had services, the people would walk for hours to get to the small church to enjoy a long service with lots of singing. Their music was heavenly. They made their own instruments: fiddles, harps and guitars. They sat sometimes for three or more hours on hard, backless benches, listening to sermons and singing praises to the Lord, often music that they had composed themselves.

When we went on a caravan to this area, we had someone sitting on the hood of the car reading the cattle tracks and other signs to direct our vehicles through the tall grass. We could not see over the grass, and our guides helped us make our own trails; surprisingly to us, we always arrived at our destination. The people would see the moving grass and dust clouds and were already arriving by the time we approached our destination.

* * * *

Joey Mendoza, a Colombian Christian Psychologist, has helped so many of our people. He worked with Sylvia, a young mother with nine children, who was very depressed. Her husband would use all the money he could beg, borrow or steal to consume alcohol. When there was no food on the table or he was drunk, which was most of the time, he became abusive. Sylvia came to know the Lord, and her life began to change. We helped her attend a Christian camp and she returned positive and radiant. She said that it was the most wonderful time of her life. She began depending on the Lord, and not on people, to solve her problems. Soon, her husband died of a massive stroke, and Sylvial was able to stand up to all the circumstances and to emerge as a leader in her community.

* * * *

During an Evangelistic Campaign in the barrio of Los Angelitos, a Colombian Baptist pastor changed his sermon at the last minute to dynamically address the problem of witchcraft and astrology that was prevalent in that neighborhood. There were twenty-five professions of faith that night. We pray for the continuing discipleship of those who made decisions and for continuing light in the previous darkness of Los Angelitos.

* * * *

In 1986, our daughter, Jennifer, was asked to sing and play the part of Mary in the local Christmas pageant. People were talking about the Baptist missionary kid who played the Virgin Mary in a Catholic-sponsored city-wide Christmas pageant.

* * * *

Our families were always worried whenever they heard news about the violence in Colombia. I was writing to them trying to relieve their anxiety, when the house suddenly shook. A car bomb had exploded nearby at the entrance of a big hotel. You could always be in the wrong place at the wrong time and encounter problems. We were told to be very vigilant of our surroundings and to avoid routines so people could not predict our schedules.

* * * *

When our daughter, Jennifer was sixteen, we asked if she would like to go with us to the Chocó. The Chocó is a large, dense, rain forrest where Colombia borders Panama. There are no roads. The only travel is by river. Most of the villages are on the bank of the river and the people have to continually use machetes to hack out the encroaching jungle. They have no electricity, no running water, (in large fiberglass tanks, they collect rain water for drinking and cooking) and their bathrooms are floating outhouses. The people are decended from freed and/ or escaped slaves that the Spaniards brought from Africa to build their forts and the city of Cartagena. Because of the excessive rainfall, 400 inches annually, the only crops that will grow are plaintains and cassava (yucca). The people make their living by selling these crops plus fishing and lumbering. Built on stilts, their homes are rustic, unpainted lumber, cut at the local sawmill. The sawmills use gasoline chain saws. It was amazing to watch two men cut straight boards off of a log, using an eight foot, two-handed rip-saw.

In the first village, La Loma, in the mornings, Jennifer helped us in surgery, and in the afternoons, she had a vacation Bible school (VBS) for about fifty children. She was a natural teacher and had a wonderful rapport with the children. Jennifer is tall, has a very pale complexion, light-colored hair and blue eyes; the children were all short and were a beautiful, blue-black color. The children surrounded her everywhere she went. She was like the Pied Piper. She slept with Elena and her mother. Jennifer was always very picky about her food, and she was a little concerned about the meals in La Loma. Elena had worked as a maid for us for several years while she studied nursing, and so knew Jennifer's likes and dislikes. With their limited supplies, they managed to provide food that she would eat. We were proud that she did not complain and tried to be a good sport about the difficulties and discomforts. Since there was no electrictiy in the village, our light source for surgery was someone holding a flashlight. This was Jennifer's job and then she helped me clean instruments afterwards. After this experience, she decided that the medical field was not for her.

We stayed in La Loma for four days and then traveled to Napipí. This pueblo is more primitive than La Loma, and the people did not seem to be interested in improving their conditions. The first day there, Jennifer suffered from Montezuma's revenge. After a trip to the "bathroom", (the floating outhouse), Jennifer looked out the window of the room where we were working, and she started to gag. She gasped that "she could not take it." We looked outside and saw a little boy standing on the side of the floating outhouse. He dipped his cup into the river and drank the water where she had just been.. The cultural shock, the smells, the attitude, the food, the conditions were too much for her to handle.

Floating outhouse in Chocó. Notice the women washing dishes and preparing food while someone is inside relieving himself or herself. Also notice the slippery plank that must be crossed to reach the bathroom.

*   *   *   *

After fourteen years in Colombia, I was excited that our church was finally going to hold a Vacation Bible School (VBS). This year, they wanted me to be the Women's missionary union (WMU) president, and I finally consented on one condition—that they would have a VBS. They agreed, and we planned a workshop to train teachers and workers. Ligia, our new pastor's wife, was to be the director. She trained the workers for the children aged 3-5, Jennifer trained the workers for children aged 6-8, and I led the conferences for children aged 9-15.

We had a good response from the workers and planned for seventy children. The first day of VBS, we enrolled one hundred fifty children, and we ended the week with two hundred fifty children in attendance. The workers were so excited about the response that they have continued a yearly VBS; they also have worked in VBS in our various missions.

A couple of weeks before the VBS was to begin, our National Convention of Baptist Churches was to be held in Cartagena, which is only a couple of hours from where we live. All the missionaries were going except Becky Dorcey and me. Since Jennifer was graduating from high school and leaving to study in the States, I wanted to stay behind and spend some special time with her.

A couple of nationals were riding with missionaries Jeni H. and Kay B. to attend the convention when they had an accident just outside of Barranquilla in which the jeep rolled over. One of the nationals was killed, and Jeni and Kay were severely injured. Someone recognized them when they were brought into a local hospital; they transferred them to our clinic, and someone called me. Robert was on his way to Cartagena; there were no cell phones at that time, so I left a message at the hotel where he was to stay, but he couldn't get back for several hours. The clinic staff was marvelous. All the doctors and nurses made themselves available to attend to Jeni and Kay. Those who were not directly involved with their care did other things. Dr. Lewis took me to *transito** (Department of Public Safety) where I retrieved the keys and other things of value that survived the crash. The jeep was a total loss, and it was a miracle that anyone survived. Someone else went with me to borrow a ventilator from another clinic, since all of ours were in use. Another person accompanied me to the police station to file an official report. Both women had received blows to the head and never remembered the details of the crash. Jeni suffered a fractured pelvis and head trauma and was kept in ICU on a ventilator. Kay had severe head trauma and was kept in ER under observation for a while; she later went home with Becky Dorsey.

While I was trying to do everything that needed to be done, Jennifer stayed at home manning the phone and keeping everyone informed. I had to call Jeni's parents and the Foreign Mission Board to report the accident. Becky called Kay's mother. Jeni's sister and brother-in-law were able to come a few days later and stayed with us until her parents could get plane reservations. J.D. and Winnie, Jeni's parents, arrived the day that Jeni was taken off the ventilator. They were able to talk to her before settling in at our home. While we were talking around the kitchen table, the clinic called, and Robert had to leave. He asked me to help him open the garage door so that he could tell me quietly, without letting her folks hear, that Jeni had suffered a pulmonary arrest.. He rushed to the clinic in less that five minutes when it usually took about fifteen. He called me later and explained that they had to put Jeni back on the ventilator. Robert stayed by her bedside all night. I let her folks have a good night's rest and told them in the morning what had happened. I was so happy that they had been able to talk with her the night before. J.D. and Winnie stayed with us for almost a month until

Jeni was stabilized enough to air evacuate back to the States. Jeni took medical leave but was back working with us in less than a year.

Kay B. had only arrived in the country in November before the accident in January. She went home for a short medical leave to recover from the traumatic beginning of her missionary career. When she returned, she was instrumental in planning and equipping the new Intensive Care Unit and training all its personnel to work there. It was the best ICU in the country. Kay accompanied us on a mobile medical trip before Jeni returned. She worked hard on this trip but felt guilty for not enjoying the primitive working conditions. I told her not to feel guilty because each of us has been given special gifts and strengths. I personally would have gone bananas working in the ICU, but I enjoyed the mobile clinics.

* * * *

In 1989, there was a Hollywood-style escape from the Metropolitan Hospital. One of the drug cartel members, had been in ICU for one month after an appendectomy. (We never understood why he was in ICU for a month!) A corporal in the army drugged the coffee of the four guards, drugged the nurse, provided an army uniform for the patient, and they all walked out and were never heard from again.

* * * *

An excerpt from a letter I wrote to a friend in 1989: ... We had a mobile medical clinic planned to San Marcos this month but have had to cancel all trips. As you have probably heard, the situation here is not good. It hasn't reached Barranquilla yet, but Medellín is reminiscent of prohibition days and organized crime. All of our missionaries there had to evacuate, leaving all their household goods behind. We can't go out of the city, even to Cartagena or Santa Marta. For several days, we were advised to stay indoors, to not even get on the street. The American Woman's Club canceled all activities. The situation is tense, and the Colombians themselves are saying that they are frightened. Robert used his time of enforced confinement to do a lot of bird-carving and painting. I have started organizing material for my book, and I am also putting a cookbook together for my kids. I hope to have it finished by this Christmas.

I had to go to the children's school the other day, and they told me that there is not one North American student left. They all left the country. The president of the American Women's Club was the wife of the U.S. Consul, and she had to leave immediately. I think the only North American club members here are those married to Colombians and me.

* * * *

In 1990, President George H. W. Bush arrived in Cartagena, Colombia for a meeting. The American Consulate advised all American citizens to keep a low profile. There was a possibility that the drug cartel or guerrillas would kidnap Americans in order to embarrass the Colombian government. In the interior of the country, there were three kidnappings. The coast observed tight security to protect all the visiting presidents. The CBS affiliate from Dallas sent their anchorman and cameraman to cover the meeting. Before arriving, they contacted our mission board and asked for our help. The two T.V. guys spent all day Sunday with us filming and interviewing us for a series of presentations. The first presentation, we found out later, was an interview with Robert and me; the second showed me playing the piano in a local church. When Jennifer heard this, I don't think that she ever stopped laughing. (I am not the greatest pianist, and our piano sounds tinny like a Honky-Tonk piano) Of all the things that they filmed, it surprised us that these were the items that they chose to show viewers in Dallas. It seemed ridiculous to us. At first, we said that we did not want to be on camera; many Colombians have satellite dishes, and you certainly can't keep a low profile if your picture is plastered in everyone's living room. They assured us it was only for the local CBS station in Dallas

* * * *

Two days after the Presidents left the country, we left for a mobile medical trip to Sucre. We stayed for only four days but managed to do forty-four surgeries—fifteen of them on the last day, and we still didn't have time to attend everyone. It rained hard on our last night, and we knew that we had to leave or we would not be able to get out. We had driven into the area in four-wheel-drive vehicles over plowed fields because it was still the dry season, but the rainy season started early and we did not want to be stuck there with our vehicles. On the return journey we did get stuck several times and had to keep pulling the jeep out of the gumbo-mud using ropes. I was wearing a divided skirt and knee-high rubber boots. As I was pulling on the rope, my boot got stuck in the mud and my foot came out of the boot, throwing me off balance, and I fell backwards. The mud sucked me down, and I felt like "Brer Rabbit and the Tar Baby." Some of the local men came running to help. I was so stuck that I pulled a couple of them in with me. We were all laughing so hard by then that it was even more difficult to be pulled out of the miry mud. No one wanted me to get back in the jeep in such a muddy state, so several ladies made a tent using sheets and I changed clothes behind it.

*   *   *   *

In 1990, the guerrillas were very active blowing up the main electric towers. Our city experienced a severe rationing of electricity. In January, we were rationed seven hours of lights a day and only had city water come in three—four days a week. We had to plan our day around these inconveniences. Fortunately, it was the breezy season and the strong trade winds kept things from becoming unbearably hot. The National Convention of the Baptist churches was being held in Barranquilla. We had two national pastors and their wives staying in our apartment for the convention. Rosenburg and Omira were from Medellín, which is up in the mountains with very cool, dry weather. Jorge and Ligia were from Armenia, also up in the mountains, but they had lived in Barranquilla for many years and were accustomed to the heat and humidity. We had no A/C, only ceiling fans in our home, and of course, the fans didn't work without electricity. Omira was suffering from the heat, and after lunch decided to shower and shampoo her hair. She went to the bathroom, and shortly afterward called out, *Socorrro!** The water had gone off, and she was lathered up from head to toe. We all knew that the lights were off, but had not thought about the water. We had large underground water storage tanks with an electric pump to pump water up to the tanks on the rooftop before it entered the house. When the tanks on the roof emptied, there was no electricity to pump more water up to fill them. I always kept a big barrel of water in the washroom on the patio, so Ligia and I formed a water brigade and hauled water and rinsed Omira off. We all had a good laugh. They are all dear friends. They call us their *gringo** parents, and their children call us their *gringo** grandparents.

Chapter 4

▼

A Grandes Males, Grandes Remedios

(Great needs require great solutions)

After the Gulf War in 1991, Robert and I spent the month of June working as medical volunteers in a Kurdish refugee camp in northern Iraq. The following are excerpts from Robert' journal about our experiences in Iraq:

We left June 3 on Lufthansa airlines from Dallas to Frankfurt, Germany. It was a very short night. We followed the channel coast of England, crossed just west of Dover, and on to Frankfurt. We changed planes and left for Ankara, Turkey, again on Lufthansa. It was cloudy most of the way, but we were able to see Istanbul and the Black Sea.

We arrived in Ankara in the evening exhausted and we collapsed into bed. Next morning, we took a taxi to the bus station where we caught a bus to the airport. We flew to Diyarbakir on Turkish Air. Ma'met, the Kurdish driver and his helper, hired by G.P (Global Partners), picked us up at the airport. We traveled four hours by car on the "Great Silk Road" to the Iraqi border. (Picture this: Four large adults crammed into a small car; Dolores and I holding our luggage in our laps and being serenaded for four hours by loud Arabic music blaring out of the speakers.)

The roads are very good, we averaged 80 MPH. We passed through Mardin, a city that sits high on a hill overlooking the plains stretching into the southern horizon.

Soon, we were riding along the Syrian border where there were fences a mere 600 meters apart with mine fields inbetween. Mountains began appearing as we approached Cizre, the place where we crossed the Tigris River, which we followed for a few miles.

All this area is grain fields—no trees, but very fertile. The valley has fruit orchards and groves of poplars planted close to each other, apparently used for poles. We arrived at the border near sundown and were met by Mike Stoop, who is the coordinator for G.P., a Non Government Organization (N.G.O.) (G.P. is an autonomous group of volunteers that responds to such emergencies and has fraternal relation with the International Mission Board) (IMB)

We then went on to Zakho in Iraq. We were not registered legally in the country because the borders on the Iraq side were abandoned. The northern area is controlled by military and Kurds under auspices of U.N. The relief work is done by the N.G.O. volunteer groups. A variety of other groups provides support such as the, U.N. and Military—(U.S., Italy, France, Britain, Spain, Dutch, etc)

We arrived at the "house" in Zakho, rented by GP. We met everyone, ate, and had prayer time. There were seventeen of us at that time. Dolores slept in women's room, and I slept on the roof in a sleeping bag on an army cot. It was very cool at that time. Later, because of increasing heat, everyone slept on the roof. It was true communal living.

We woke up next morning early. The flies land on your nose and forehead at 4:45 a.m. when the sun is just coming up. There is prayer call at 3:00 AM. broadcasted from the Mosque which we heard the first night only.

We ate breakfast, and everyone fixes his own. There is cereal, milk, juice, hot water and instant coffee. We left at 6:45 for Camp II and OutPatient Department. We worked in three 2-pole army tents. At that time, we had three Kurdish Doctors, plus Dr. Niel, Dr. Bassan Haskim, and, Dr. Hincheran. Dr. Niel, is a retired ENT doctor, Dr. Haskim is an infectious disease specialist from Washington, D.C. and is a second generation Arab. Dr. Hincheran is the daughter-in-law of Dr. Niel. She is a Turkish anesthesiologist. Also working with us: Dr. Bill Skinner, retired Baptist missionary from Paraguay; Dr. Lee Baggett, missionary from Guadalajara, Mexico; volunteer Joann Broadus, head of OB nursing at University of South Alabama's School of Nursing (U.S.A.), who did the gynecology—(Kurdish women will not allow men to examine them); volunteer Dr. Alice Ward, professor of nursing at U.S.A.; Judy Wise, RN, missionary nurse from Mexico, who scrounged and made tent visits; Donna Rye, RN, missionary from Mexico, who worked in medicine and assisted in Women's tent; Steve Edwards, missionary (no kin except in the Lord's family), also from Mexico who administered the OPD (outpatient department); Todd Bennett and Gary Stroop, gof-

ers; and Todd Augustine, who cooked for us. Several others left the day after we got there. There were several Kurds hired to triage, interpret, and control the flow.

Our workday, at first, was eight till about one, then two to five, in the afternoon we were half-strength so some could rest. We worked seven days a week, off Friday and Sunday afternoons for respective Holy days—Muslim and Christian. The schedule changed from time to time, due mostly to increasing heat. As we were leaving because of decreasing load and increasing heat, we cut out afternoons all together.

The personnel turned over frequently. The house we lived in was not finished well inside. There was some furniture in the living room. There was a Turkish toilet (called a squatty potty by the group). We had two port-a-potties, and with such a crowd, they had to be emptied frequently. When the Turkish toilet stopped up, we had to empty the port-a-potties in plastic bags and take them to the dump,(a dry riverbed) and shoo the garbage-picking kids away. When they finally realized what it was, they left.

The Army provided most of our provisions. They also put in flooring for our tents. The army and marines did an excellent job. We ate food provided by Army and others, supplemented by vegetables and fruits bought in local markets—excellent, but limited in variety. We ate MRE's for lunch usually. Meal Ready to Eat—(how to describe)—they filled your tummy and were adequate, but we were all happier when we started preparing something else for lunch.

There was an abundance of snack foods. When Todd (our cook) left, the women in the group took turns cooking the evening meal. When it was your turn, you had the afternoon off (???) to do the washing, marketing, and cooking the meal on a gas hotplate for eleven to seventeen people. Needless to say, we welcomed Virginia Smith with open arms when she arrived and took over this duty.

We had cases of water in plastic 1.5 liter bottles, which we kept refrigerated (by mid morning, these were boiling hot in the tents at camp). We each had to drink at least two to three bottles a day just to replace the liquid that we lost due to the extreme heat.

The diseases we saw were what one would expect to find in a refugee situation with the history of having fled to, and survived, a mountainous region in winter with nothing but the clothes on their backs. There were a lot of stress related illnesses, amenorrhea*, anxiety, peptic ulcers, etc. A lot of illness related to the hardship and coldweather, several cases of Bell's palsy*, foot trauma, old frostbite, exacerbation of arthritis and rheumatism. In taking a medical history, the norm would be, "When did it start?" ... "Three months ago." (When they were in the mountains). Most of these folks lived in cities or villages, and were somewhat sedentary, and not really prepared for this. How could anyone have been prepared?

There were illnesses related to crowding and sanitation. The camps were well-provided with water, latrines and food by military, etc. Typhoid, URI's*, strep throat, a lot of Hepatitis, chicken pox, measles (a few cases although every child who came in camp was supposed to have been vaccinated), gastroenteritis, (the dehydration augmented by the severe heat, up to 114° F. and rising daily), malnutrition, otitis, scabies, conjunctivitis due to the hot blowing sand, and occasionally brucellosis*.

There were burns, again usually three months old, related to explosions of oil/gas in houses, set off by bombings. There were also shrapnel and gunshot wounds. Bullets and bombs are no respecters of persons or age. One boy had received shrapnel to the face, destroying the conjunctiva, the sclera, and all but central part of cornea in one eye. One mother came in to have her amputated leg dressed. In trying to save her ten-year-old son, she stepped on a mine and lost her leg, as well as her son.

Later on, we began to get patients from all over northern Iraq. They came with chronic problems to see the "Famous European Doctor" (their words), looking for miracles or hoping to be able to go outside Iraq for care.

Among these were cases of paralysis due to polio, epilepsy, various neurological disorders, and amputations (many of these were left over from the Iran-Iraq war). One told me that in his city there were 200 like him needing stump revision, physical therapy, and prostheses. A lot of people came for medicines that were in short supply all over, for diabetes, hypertension etc. We were well-stocked with medicines for the most part, but a few things were in short supply.

Generally, we couldn't do much for the chronic cases. We had a hospital next door for acute care and rehydration for the camp folks. The Italian military had a hospital for referrals, but they were limited. There was a hospital in Zakho, but they were working to their limits. The hospitals in Dohuk and Mosul were other possibilities, but often people would say that they had already been there. There was almost no chance of leaving the country.

Then, there were a few patients who had been tortured. I saw one man about mid-fifties, who had been beaten severely about head and shoulders, had needles inserted, and then was submitted to electric shock. This was a year ago. As a result, he had two toes amputated and was left with bilateral partial brachial plexus palsy (damaged nerves that go to upper extremity).

The policy of the U.N., and therefore all of the groups working under it, was to "normalize" things as quickly as possible. That meant getting everyone out of the camp and into their homes. It was ideal, but the reality was that Saddam destroyed many villages where these folks lived. Other villages are without services, and others are booby-trapped. GP hopes to help reestablish water supplies. The people have to be in permanent—type shelters by the winter, or they won't survive.

The northern part of Iraq is controlled by the U.N. and the Peshmerga (the Kurdish military), supported up to now by multinational military. Due to this the Iraqis are not present in this area; in order to be legally in the country, we had to go to Mosul (Nineveh) which is Iraq-controlled to get our visas. After waiting in the heat there all morning, we understood why Jonah went the other way!

We traveled as a group under protection of the U.N. security, and there were no problems. Previously, there were rumors that we would have to go to Bagdad or send our passports (which we were told we would not do by the U.S. authorities in the area). There was considerable concern among the relief workers.

A lot of this would have been difficult to take had it not been for the realization that God had a purpose in our being there, and that we could go to Him with our cares.

One of the beautiful experiences we had was our prayer time every night. Sometimes, it was delayed because of finishing late at OPD; sometimes, we finished at 8:00 PM, then supper, baths, washing clothes, etc.—but each night, we would get together to express concerns, requests, praises and pray together. Then sleep, blessed sleep!

The Kurds are a friendly and gentle people, intelligent with a good sense of humor. Most of the ones we got to know well, including the interpreters, their families, merchants in the city, and neighbors, were well-educated, and mostly middle-class. I had three interpreters while I was there: Arif, Muhsin, and Yaseen (the first two only a short time). Muhsin is a graduate engineer; the other two still are studying. Yaseen is a sixth-year medical student who is afraid he will be unable to finish, because all doctors after school, owe five years of military service as a soldier in Saddam's army.

We were invited to Yaseen's house for lunch. He lives in Zakho with his aunt's family—aunt, uncle, another uncle, and 13 kids. We sat on the floor in the parlor, (mercifully they had an evaporative cooler) and ate a spread of dishes: large pilaf with raisins, nuts, dates, a dish of ribs with vegetables, fish with vegetables, Dolmas (stuffed grape leaves, squash, etc.) stuffed with rice and spices, and goat yogurt to drink.

It was all delicious, and later, we were served fruit and tea. Tea is served hot and sweet in a glass on a saucer, and is very good. It is served all day on any occasion. If you enter a shop or market, you are served tea. The meal was delicious, and the visit was wonderful. Normally, the women do not eat with the men, but in Dolores' honor, they permitted two of the young women in the family to eat with us. We had forgotten to bring our camera, so we had to return another afternoon for photos. They dressed us in typical costumes, and we all took pictures. This family, like all the others—thirteen kids and all—had to flee to the mountains. When they discovered that our living quarters did not have air-conditioning they tried to get us to move in with them, and they would give us their only air-conditioned room as our own. All things considered, it was tempting, but we said that we had to stay with our group.

One of the highlights was a Friday afternoon excursion of all of us and the Kurdish workers to the waterfall across the Valley to the northeast into the mountains. There is a waterfall about fifty meters high, shaded and very cool. It has a picnic area and stairways leading to different levels. We brought chicken breast (canned and compliments of U.S. Army) to barbecue, potato salad, and the Kurds brought Dolmas. We ate, danced and had a wonderful visit.

The men line up, hold little fingers and dance around in a circle. The one on the lead end holds a leafy branch in his right hand. They sing folk songs as they dance.

The Kurds we worked with were curious about our beliefs. We shared with them on a personal basis as much as possible, realizing the great social and legal difficulties, as well as cultural, for them to become Christians. We were forbidden to initiate any witness, but we could respond.

There is a Christian quarter in Zakho—a Caldean church (that we visited) and a Syrian Church. The Christians cannot, and do not, proselytize. (The Priest told us that if a Christian began socializing with a Muslin, the Muslin family would have the couple killed. It was illegal, but the authorities would look the other way.)

Many of the Kurds look upon us as their saviors. They thank us and are eager to give us gifts such as scrumptous fruits.. Dolores had a woman kiss her hands and arms, blessing her saying, "May you live two hundred years." We pray that one day they may come to know the real Savior.

Our last day of work, one of the translators brought us a picture of an old bridge in Zakho said to have been constructed in 2073 B.C. On the back, he had written these words: "Dear Robert and Dolores, besides being an excellent Doctor and Nurse, you are kindhearted people who come to help miserable people. I respect you and appreciate your hard work. I will remember you all my life and pray for you. God bless you and God be with you. Yours sincerely L."

* * * *

Sue, a volunteer from England, and I were doing tent visits with patients who could not make it to the clinics. One of our patients was in tremendous pain from injuries due to torture he had received from Saddam's men. Every time that he was moved he would scream and pass out. Sue and I enlisted help from some Dutch corpsmen and used their ambulance to take the patient to the French Army Hospital for treatment. We then had to instruct the wife how to do the home treatment because Sue and I were women, and infidels to boot, and we could not touch him. Working through our interpreter, we taught the wife what to do. Sue was so moved by his condition that she asked the couple, through our interpreter, if she could pray for them. The interpreter got very angry and yelled that they did not want or need our prayers. "If Alla willed it, the man would live. If Alla willed it, the man would die." I whispered to Sue that we did not need their permission to pray and to hold her tongue for now. We all prayed for them in our group prayer time that night. Two weeks later, that man walked into our clinic on crutches. He and his wife wanted to thank us.

One day at noon, as the volunteer group was returning to the group house for lunch and a short rest, I was late getting to the truck. Everyone began shouting, "Dolores!, Hurry Dolores!" As I went running toward the truck, a young U.S. soldier, who was working in the tent next to ours, called out to me, "Ma'am, Is your name Dolores?" When I said yes, he came over and said that his mother's name was Dolores, and he really was missing her. He asked if I would give him a hug. My heart went out to him. He was so young and lonely. I hugged him as if he were my own and told him that we were proud of him and that God loved him.

* * * *

We received a letter from one of our Kurdish translators, Shawkat, telling about the changes in Iraq after we left. Shawkat worked as a nurse assistant for us in the clinics. He continued working with the Global Partners after we left but later got a job at the hospital in Dohuk. We heard that later he was on the helicopter that was shot down by friendly fire over northern Iraq. He was acting as translator for some of the military personnel, and he died along with others on the helicopter.

CHAPTER 5

La Necesidad Abre la Puerta de Muchos Logros

(Necessity is the mother of invention)

These were the days before computers and e-mail in Colombia. I got my first computer in the late '90s; a little later, when the phone service became more reliable, I got my e-mail. During the first few years we sometimes had to wait fifteen minutes to get a dial tone. If we were lucky, the lines were not crossed, sending us to a wrong number, making us start all over again. We would laugh when we watched an old movie that showed someone in a foreign country pick up a phone and immediately get a call through to the States. It was certain that they had never been in Colombia. Mail service was almost as bad. The Foreign Mission Board sent a letter asking us to meet an official of the Women's Missionary Union who had a long layover in Barranquilla. We received the letter more than five months after she had come and gone.

* * * *

In 1992, I had the opportunity to provide a program about our medical caravan work to the American Woman's Club in Barranquilla. The newly arrived wife of the American Consul was present, afterwards, she mentioned that it was hard for her to understand why we had chosen to live here for eighteen years. They were not allowed to stay in Barranquilla for more than three years because of the difficult living conditions, the rigors of the hot, humid climate, and the security. I told her that many years ago I had chosen a beautiful place to live (Lake Jackson, Texas) and was very happy, content, and comfortable living there for six years; but God had other plans for me. When you live where God wants you to live and do what He wants you to do, He gives you the strength and ability to make something positive out of your circumstances. We came to love the people in Colombia.

* * * *

Robert came home one day with tears in his eyes, very touched by one of his patients. He wrote the following:

Two Eggs

This morning, Emilia brought me two eggs.—Big deal?—YES!—Emilia is from a small fishing village about 35 miles from Barranquilla. She is the town "mother"— seeing that everybody in town (most of whom are kin) gets what he needs.

We began working with this village in the mid-1970's. We did not see much progress, and after ten years, we left. Others went. In the last couple of years, the seed has born fruit. There is a very active congregation led mostly by Emilia's nephew. That church has its own mission in a nearby town.

After we left, the sick were brought to Barranquilla by bus to be seen in my office. Economically, the town does not have very much. Emilia often brought me fish, shrimp or oysters (very tiny) for payment. This morning, Emilia brought me two eggs. They were very carefully wrapped in dried palm leaves, tied at each end to form a sort of cradle. There has been no fish, and I guess, precious little else there. Emilia brought me two eggs. One of the most precious gifts I have ever received.

* * * *

We don't always have the opportunity to see the results of the testimony of our MK's (missionary kids). I was unable to drive for a few months due to a back problem and had to take taxis everywhere. I had a marvelous experience with a driver the other day. I didn't recognize him, but he immediately asked me how Jennifer was (our youngest daughter). He said that he had been her school bus driver for many years. He always thought that she was a beautiful young lady and her personality radiated such beauty and happiness; he asked what her beauty secret was. She said that it was her relationship with the Lord. For several days, he asked her to sit up front and talked with her. He realized that he did not have any relationship with the Lord, and he began seeking. He now has found the Lord and is attending a local church. He asked that I tell Jennifer that Elías sends his love and his gratitude for sharing her beauty secret.

* * * *

One Wednesday night, a young woman, Nydia, and her two small children were passing by the mission during our Bible study. They came in and sat in the back of the room. After the study, Nydia came forward and said that after sitting down, she realized that she had made a mistake—this was not where she had planned on going, but she had been too embarrassed to get up and leave. She was so excited and asked if she could come back; she had never heard anything so exciting. She did come back and came to know the Lord in a personal way.

* * * *

We returned to Barranquilla in 1993 to a warm welcome after a brief furlough in the States. The temperature was 95°F with 85% humidity. Sunday was to be a day of national census; therefore, everyone had to stay in their homes or be arrested. Only doctors and other specially-named people who had special government permits could leave their homes during a twenty-four-hours period beginning at midnight on Saturday until midnight on Sunday. Even the airports were closed. Our churches had their services on Saturday night. Several people asked if we were glad to be back. Robert and I laughed and replied that in spite of stepping off the plane and being hit with the hot/humid tropical heat, in spite of the typical wild taxi ride where you literally hang onto your seat, in spite of the necessary papers needed to be able to drive our car being lost in the mail, in spite of trying unsuccessfully to call Bogotá after two hours of trying, in spite of the report that human feces have been found in the cities drinking water, in spite of the fact that our ceiling fan went out this morning, that yes, we were glad to be back because this is where the Lord wanted us to be. He didn't promise that it would be easy but He is with us at all times. National brethren were calling welcoming us back. Our neighbors had flowers on the table and came to visit. The relaxation that we need is being provided,—not in the way we would have chosen, but we couldn't leave the house all day Sunday. The Lord blesses us in so many ways.

The music program in our local church continues to grow. As the church pianist, I have to practice a lot to be able to play the cantatas that we perform at Easter and Christmas. Every Sunday there are one or two people who want to sing specials. This is fine, when I have advanced warning. But several times, someone approaches me Sunday morning, right as the services are about to begin, and wants me to accompany them in a solo with a hymn that I have never heard before; they proceed to hum it to me, and without any practice, we perform. We are getting a reputation now for having a fine choir and have received several invitations to sing in various churches. We also performed our cantata in a big park on Good Friday. In a couple of places, I had to accompany the choir on instruments that I had never played before, such as an electric piano—the type used to play rock music—and it only had one volume: LOUD. For a person who doesn't know music very well I'm learning to fake it so that most people, here at least, can't tell.

We had a mobile medical caravan planned for November, but it was looking "iffy." The pastor in the area called and said that the guerrillas had been to visit several times asking when we were to arrive. The guerrillas had a number of their men with new and old wounds and other illnesses. The pastor did not think that it would be wise for us to go at that time.

* * * *

In September 1994, we traveled back to the States for our daughter Barbara's wedding to Joe Sanderson. The WMU at Trinity Baptist Church in Kerrville adopted Barbara and gave her a wedding shower. They prepared all the little rice bags and also served at the wedding reception. We were so grateful since we could not be there for the pre-wedding arrangements.

* * * *

An excerpt from letter to Jeni Hester November 1994: ... Our phone has been out since August. The phone company finally sent someone to check the line and found that our neighbor across the street had redirected our line to their house.

We just returned from a caravan to Miraflores. Sandy and Nancy attended about four hundred patients in four and a half working days, and Robert saw seventy-nine and did twenty-seven surgeries. He came down with dengue fever on the trip out; he was very sick, but kept working. He bathed himself in repellant to keep the mosquitoes from biting him and transmitting the disease to others. He didn't do as much as usual, as you can see from the statistics. He had to lie down after each case. He had 104° fever and terrific bone pain, eye pain and weakness. Rafael Blanco could not get off work to go with us, and he was to have taught a conference on discipleship. I filled in for him and taught the conference during the Sunday School hour. Since Robert was too sick to bring the message, I did that also. I finally talked Robert into going home, and Tulio arranged for the canoe to pick us up a day earlier than expected.

The team was able to return to the Chocó after a six-year absence. Because of my back spasms, Robert wouldn't let me go. Thank Goodness! They went by bus to Medellín, then by bus from Medellín to Quibdó (big mistake). It took thirteen hours to travel only 80 miles on a road that even Robert said was terrible. Everyone was throwing up and bruised from being thrown around in the bus. They arrived in Quibdó and found a 5 star hotel to rest for a few hours. The next morning, they decided that maybe it was a .5 star hotel, but at the time, it had running water and the bed didn't move. They hired a fast boat to take them to Vigía del Fuerte to await Elena who had gone on a river boat from Cartagena. It took her four days, but they all decided that it was a better way of getting there. They found a few faithful believers still meeting, but without direction. Robert took them and did a discipleship course, and José DeMoya did the evangelistic service. It was exciting to have two of the young people from our church, Geraldo Escobar, a dentist, and Nancy Jaraba, a doctor, to accompany Robert. These young people were good friends of Jennifer and sang with her in a youth group. Now, they are both professionals, helping out with the caravan work. On the way back, they decided to get a charter plane from Vigía to Medellín. It seemed at first to be more expensive. They found out later that Quibdó was celebrating Carnival. There were no available hotels or transportation out of Quibdó, so they did well to just get back. At 6:00 AM, they rang my doorbell and asked if I would please fix them breakfast—anything that wasn't *plátano** or *borojó.** We had a caravan scheduled to go to Minca (a small pueblo in the mountains of Sierra Nevada about two hours from where we lived), but we had to cancel because of security problems. There was a picture in the paper of armored trucks on the road up to Minca where the guerrillas and the army had a confrontation with bombs and mortars. It is calm at the moment, but we are not going up anytime soon.

This has not been a good year in regards to health. First, the back spasms that laid me low, then tooth abscesses. The abscess that I had at mission meeting did more damage than we thought. One dentist tried to redo a root canal, but found that the root had a hairline fracture and it had to be pulled. It was the front bottom incisor, so he decided I needed a tooth implant and sent me to another specialist. He did the surgery and found that the abscess had destroyed a large portion of the bone so had to also put in a bone substitute. He did a panoramic x-ray and said that I needed to have two other root canals redone and ten crowns replaced. Jeni, you know how I hate to go to the dentist. The Lord used all of this to make me stop and rethink my ministry and change some of what I was doing. I was able to finish a cookbook of our family recipes that I had promised to make for the kids but never seemed to have the time to do. It turned out rather well and a lot bigger that we had anticipated.

* * * *

In 1994, one block from the house, a woman ran a stop sign and hit the passenger side of our jeep, spinning it around, and turning it over. The crowd of people that gathered around helped pull Robert out of the over turned car. Someone recognized Robert and called the clinic, which sent an ambulance for their beloved doctor. Twelve people from the clinic crammed into the amulance (slight over-kill) to assist. Fortunately, no one was injured, but Robert had to go to the police station where they towed his car. The red tape involved in an accident is very time-consuming. While he went to the police station, the ambulance, with all its people, came to the house to inform me of the accident. I watched the ambulance pull up to the front of the house. As the ambulance driver, plus the clinic chaplain, slowly walked to the front door, my heart sank. They all began to speak at once, explaining, "He's ok. He's ok. The car is a mess but he is fine."

The woman who caused the accident did not have insurance. The mission decided it was better to spend $3,000.00 U.S. to fix our 1983 Toyota than to pay $22,000.00 U.S. to buy a used 1986 Toyota that had the same milage. Richard, our car coordinator did not think that it was in much better shape mechanically than our damaged car ...

* * * *

An excerpt from letter to parents November 1994 ... We will be on a medical caravan during Thanksgiving so our usual turkey and dressing will be exchanged for turkey soup. Oh well, we will have to wait until Christmas this year.

Aida (our maid) has been going to school all this year, and hopefully, she will get her high school diploma if she passes her exams next week. She dropped out of school to go to work to help her family. She turned thirty-one this past June, and we have been encouraging her to finish her education. She now wants to attend the university by correspondence. I hope that she can do this; she is too good a girl to spend the rest of her life doing domestic work for lack of an education.

We have been watching a lot of American football. Barbara and Joe sent us several VCR tapes of the games, and we have enjoyed them even though they are several weeks old. We miss not being able to see sports on T.V., but we don't have time to sit and watch a whole game anyway. This way we can watch part of a game and return to it when we have more time.

* * * *

April 1995:... The team of nine arrived in Los Cargueros and were taken to different homes where we were to stay for the week of the medical caravan. We had a few minutes to lie down to rest before we had to go to a wedding that Rafael Blanco, the chaplain at our clinic, was going to perform. When we arrived at the church, we almost fell off the bench laughing when we realized that Robert and I were staying at the bride and groom's house and sleeping in the matrimonial bed. They were wed on Monday night, and they were baptized on Thursday. What a beautiful way to start their life together.

* * * *

After our annual mission meeting in 1996, Sandy G., the Ruede family, Eslie P., a Colombian family, and Robert and I flew from Bogotá to Leticia, which is on the Amazon, for some vacation time. Our guide was a character named Chiri-Chiri, and his helper was Juan. They were excellent. We had to delay the start because of strong winds and extreme cold. You think of heat when you go to the Amazon, right? We thought that we had made a mistake and had arrived in Alaska. They were having an unexpected cold wave, and we all nearly froze to death the first three days and nights. We slept in all our clothes, plus rain coats and still froze. The "hotel" where we stayed the first night did not have blankets, only giving us a thin bottom and top sheet for the beds. The windows had screens but no glass or wood panes, so we had open ventilation. We considered sleeping all together for body heat. The second night, we stayed in some private cabañas.

They were built on a high bluff overlooking the river and beautifully landscaped. Ten of us slept in the same one—room cabaña and shared a bathroom. Again, it was cold. The Jimenez family were from Bogotá, which is cold most of the time; they said they never wore even sweaters in Bogotá, but they were freezing along with the rest of us. At the cabañas there was a monkey and a Macaw that were pets and kept jumping on the heads, shoulders and backs of the people. The kids thought it was fun; the adults weren't too excited about it. Our group was planning a three-hour hike through tough jungle trails. The guide described it as a hard up-and-down trail while crossing logs and mucking through lots of mud. Those not wanting to make the arduous hike could travel with the boat to the next pueblo to meet the team in three hours. I decided to go with the boat and I am glad that I did. Some of the group had a hard time on the trail thinking that they would not make it. All came back muddy, some more so that others, having fallen into the mud several times. They were exhausted. One of the things that everyone wanted to see was the pink dolphins that live in the Amazon river. Because of the cold, we had not seen any until that afternoon. While on the boat, the guide, driver and I ran into a school of dolphins and stopped to watch them roll and play for about fifteen minutes. We arrived at the pueblo of San Martín where about four hundred Ticuna Indians live. The guide took me to visit in the homes of all the Indians, and they were so hospitable. He left me in the care of the Indians while he went to look for the group as they finished their hike. The Indian woman where I stayed introduced me to her fifteen-year-old daughter. She was concerned because the girl wasn't married. They have puberty rites for the girls at thirteen years of age and then the girls marry. This girl was slightly retarded, and they couldn't find a husband for her. She asked me if I had any unmarried sons, and when I said yes, she got excited and asked me to send him to her because she needed a son-in-law. I didn't know if she was serious or not, but the guide said that yes—she was very serious. I wrote to our son Charles, who was attending a university in the States, that he had received his first marriage proposal. Usually, the guide had his tour group spend the night in this village with the Indians. We had asked to stay in the national park, and we were very glad that we had. Robert and I have stayed in primitive places, but the rest of the group would have had a difficult time. In comparison, the park was luxurious. Since the river rises during the rainy season, the buildings were all built on stilts. Again, we all stayed in the same room, but we could choose a hammock or a cot to sleep on. The cots didn't look too comfortable so most of us choose a hammock. One thing we had not considered was the COLD. The cold came from all angles, and we could not get warm. Also, there was a puppy that somehow had gotten shut into the room with us. He started scratching and hitting his elbow on the floor so much that each of us, silently, was waiting for someone else to get up to let him out. It was so cold that no one wanted to move out of his cocoon and hoped that someone else would do it. Finally, Robert couldn't stand it anymore since the dog was under his hammock, so he got up and put him out. Then the puppy started whining and banging against the door. No one slept much that night. Robert got up every morning at 5:30 to watch the birds wake up. Thankfully, the puppy followed him that morning. After breakfast, we were taken on another hike through the jungle. We left later that morning to go to Brazil to eat lunch that was finally served about 4:00 PM. We got back to Leticia about 9:00 PM. Everyone was concerned because, although the boat had a spotlight, it failed, and all we had was a weak flashlight to light our way back to Leticia. The nights on the Amazon through the jungle are very dark. At least we were all provided with life vests, and this was a first for us. The day we were scheduled to return to Bogotá the flight was delayed and finally canceled, so we spent another night in Leticia. The group went looking for pink dolphins again and found them. We also went to a museum and the zoo. The guide took Robert on a last hike to see birds outside the city. They didn't see many birds but did go to another Indian village. They met the chief and were given a special tour that Robert found fascinating. The rest of us went to the small zoo where the monkeys and ant eaters roamed freely, and they followed us around the park. The next day, when we went to the museum and were learning about some of the customs and life of the Indians, Robert said that he had seen many of the items on exhibit, like the meeting hut, the log drums, and totem poles, in the village the day before.

The food was all delicious. Although we ate fish at least two times a day, it was very well-prepared and very different from any that we had ever eaten. We all enjoyed the trip very much and were ready to do it again.

* * * *

An excerpt from a letter to the Faith Bible Class in Shreveport, La. dated August 10, 1996:

... The *barrio* called Villa San Carlo began about six years ago as an invasion *barrio** (a squatter's neighborhood). A politician, without any legal authority, later "gave" the property to the people. They do not have legal, registered titles, but do have papers saying that the property is theirs. After six years, the people do have electricity, but no water or sewage. They have to buy every drop of water that they use for bathing, drinking, cleaning, and cooking. Three years ago, a volunteer group from Virginia came to hold VBS and medical clinics for a week in two different *barrios*. When they left, a fifteen-year-old young man living in this *barrio* continued to hold Bible studies for the children with an average of twenty-five children attending. The adults approached me to start a Bible study for them. The *barrio* is out on the edge of town with no street lighting, terrible roads, and poor transportation (at night time it can be dangerous). Since our church people were concerned about a lone woman going there at night, one of our church deacons met me at the entry to the *barrio*. We began meeting in the home of Hermana Victoria, and soon, we were overflowing her small home. The house next door to Victoria was up for sale. We talked to the owner, and he said that he might rent it to us for the equivalent of $80 U.S. dollars a month. We told him that if he would lower the rent to $50 we would be interested. (We really did not even have this amount, but the group said that if we could get it for this price that somehow we would find the money). He said no. Several months went by, and we were praying that the Lord would lead us to an adequate place. The day that I received word from the owner that he would rent to us for $50, I received a letter with a check for $100 from one of the original volunteers of the VBS team. She felt led to send something for the work in this *barrio*. I immediately wrote back to tell her that God had used her to answer our prayers. We had two months rent! We began meeting in the house which is large by their standards. We had a few benches; but the majority had to stand, and the children had to sit on the floor. There was enough space that the children could meet at the same time in another room. We had an average of thirty adults and forty to fifty children. The people collected offerings to buy fans. We were melting in the building that has a front door, one window, a back door, cement block walls and tin roof. The temperature here is similar to your hottest day in Shreveport in summer with very high humidity. It never changes. These people are very poor, and many do not have work. ProSalud, which is directed by one of our missionary nurses, Jeni Hester, goes to this *barrio* with a group of health promoters every two weeks for well baby clinics and nutrition programs. There are several babies and small children who are actually dying from malnutrition. We are trying to help by providing basic food and health care for the children and teaching the families how to improve their conditions as best they can in their situations.

Let me tell you about two of the young ladies who live there:

Janet is a young teen who swallowed insecticide trying to kill herself. She had failed the year in her school and was told that she could not attend next semester because there was no space for someone who had failed. Her family had sacrificed in order for her to go to school, and she felt that she had let them down.

Julia is a young woman with two small children, no work, and her husband had abandoned them. She was desperate and contemplating suicide.

We were able to counsel these two young women and show them that they were not alone. Someone cared for them. <u>God</u>! He cared enough that He sent people to help them. They have come to know the Lord as their Savior, and they now help in the different programs that we offer. Their lives now are worth living, and they serve the Lord by helping others.

The first of July, we received word from the owner of the house where we meet that he wanted us to vacate the premises by the end of the month. He wanted to open a cantina/bar/billiard hall. We sent out, via our e-mail prayer network, an urgent prayer request that we could find a suitable place to meet and that the cantina would not be opened in this area. The next day, before anyone had time to respond to the request, we began receiving love gifts in the mail. We received the exact amount of the selling price that the owner was asking for the building. We had not even dreamed of buying the place because the owner was asking $3,000 dollars, and our average offering collected for a month is about $10 dollars—enough to pay for lights and water (that they do not receive). We had been receiving special love gifts to pay the rent. God knows our needs before we do and supplies our every need.

* * * *

Barrio Villa San Carlos is a neighborhood on the outer edge of Barranquilla. Unemployment is very high. Many work in menial jobs or as day laborers if, or when, they do get work. One Christmas, we decided to have a surprise Christmas party for the children who had been attending the mission church. There were eighty enrolled. We put together gifts that consisted of one pencil, one small notebook, one small toy, one piece of candy and one cookie. We wrapped them in a plastic bag and tied each with a colorful ribbon. We prepared one hundred twenty bags knowing that we would probably have extra children come to the party. We had two hundred children show up. We gave each of our enrolled children a complete bag, and then opened the other bags and gave each of the remaining children either one pencil, one notebook, or one toy. Everyone went home with something and they were very happy. This was all that many received that Christmas.

* * * *

Daniel, member of a street gang that had been terrorizing the area, had his life completely changed after coming to know Jesus as his Savior. Daniel was sitting with his gang on a street corner in a small *barrio* when Victoria, (a local leader of the mission) and I were going to a Bible study in the home of one of the believers. Victoria walks with a crutch because of an above-the-knee amputation, but she is more agile than someone with two strong legs. She called one of the boys over to help her carry her Bible to the study in a home ten blocks away. Daniel reluctantly agreed to help her. When we arrived at the home, Victoria maneuvered Daniel inside, and then she stood in the doorway preventing him from leaving. The room was crowded with about twenty people, and Daniel tried to make himself invisible. We talked about God's Love for us. Many of the people began giving testimony of how they had experienced God's Love in their life. Daniel snorted and mumbled that God didn't love him; nobody loved him. Daniel came from a dysfunctional family and had never experienced love. We began reading scripture about God's Love, and tears began falling down Daniel's face. He said nobody loved him; his father had abandoned the family and his mother worked constantly to put food on the table. His mother, his unmarried sister and her baby, and Daniel all lived in a one-room shack with no running water, and the cooking facilities and bathroom were outside. Daniel was looking for acceptance and love within the street gang. It blew his mind when he realized that God truly did love him. He gave his heart to Jesus and wanted to know more about God and His Son. I began discipling him in his home, and he grew more and more radiant as he learned about Jesus. His life changed so much that his mother and his sister also accepted Jesus as their Savior. His neighbors were amazed at the change in him and wanted to know more. His brothers in the gang did not understand, but every time that I arrived in that barrio, they were at the entrance to greet me and escort me back to the Bible study. They would sometimes say that it was not a good day for me to go into the barrio. I took this to mean that it was dangerous at that time. I would then spend a little time with them and give each a hug, we would talk and then I would return home. I believe that God used the people to keep us safe. There were shoot outs and thievery every day, and it was possible to find yourself in the wrong place at the wrong time and get caught up in these activities. Fortunately, I was never injured.

*Daniel, a 15 year-old ex-street gang member being discipled by the author. They are studying the
Bible. Daniel is learning how to grow as a new Christian.*

* * * *

A fifty-nine-year-old woman, who was a new Christian in Villa San Carlos, was diagnosed with a malignant tumor of the uterus. Feeling that God was with her and comforting her, she took the news of the cancer well. However, the straw that broke the camel's back was the page-long list of items that the hospital required her to bring before she could be admitted and programmed for the surgery. The items included a list of all her medicines, bed sheets, I.V. fluids and I.V. tubing, syringes, sterile gloves and many other things. She was appalled that they did not even have a band-aid. She lost all confidence in the hospital, the doctors, and the system.

* * * *

The children in one of our VBS programs collected a mission offering and decided to use the money to provide a food basket for a poor family in the mission at Villa San Carlos. After buying the large basket of food, the ladies from our church decided to divide it into several smaller baskets to provide for more families. While I taught the Bible study in the front room, the ladies from our church were in the back room dividing up the basket. As I watched the mothers arrive for the Bible study with their haggard faces, each carrying a baby in arms and one or two other children holding on to the mother's dress, I wondered how we would decide who to give the baskets to. I counted forty mothers. I though that we might have to draw names out of a hat or something. After the study I went into the back room and asked how the ladies were coming along with the baskets. I had goosebumps when they said that they had forty small baskets. God again provides just what we need.

* * * *

Carnival just keeps getting wilder each year. I think that everyone is trying to drink and party themselves into a stupor so that they can forget the scandals that are going on in the government. The newspaper wrote that fifty-nine percent of the people asked said that they thought that President Samper should resign. Seventy percent thought that he was lying about his involvement with the narcos. Some think that if he does not resign that there could be a coup. The Head of the military said in an interview that the military serves the Office of the President and not the man in the Office.

* * * *

Wade and Barbara Akins returned to lead another conference teaching their manual on church planting and evangelization, "Pioneer Evangelism." Following is an excerpt from their e-mail after one of these conferences:.... *"Wow! If you ever want to meet some modern heroes of the faith go to Colombia and meet our IMB missionaries! These missionaries live in constant threats and dangers which most of us never have to think about. They all deserve our highest respect and honor and they need ALL believers around the world to pray for them and their fellow believers in Colombia.*

God is moving in Colombia in a mighty and powerful way! Revival is spreading all across the nation and especially in the northern region where we just held our most recent Pioneer Evangelism Conference.

More than 170 people attended representing 105 different churches and congregations. There was truly a revival spirit in these meetings. All were trained "how to" do evangelism and church planting. About 20% of those who attended came from the RED ZONE of Colombia. Those are the areas controlled by the guerrilla groups and no one not from there is allowed in. Yet, God is there.

Here is a true story. My interpreter's brother had been kidnapped (like so many people are every day as you all know). The guerilla groups had stolen goods off a truck but the truck had turned out to be a Gideon Bible truck. So, at their base camp in the mountains they had Communist magazines and these Gideon Bibles. He said that his brother was not a believer but after he got to the base camp he began to read the Word of God. He trusted Christ as his Lord and Savior while there. This just demonstrates the power of God!"....

* * * *

A translated excerpt from a letter written to the Director of the Baptist Clinic from the Mayor of Majagual, Sucre in February 1996 ... "We send our heartfelt thanks to Dr. Edwards and his team of health workers for the help rendered our people, who are economically poor. In appreciation for their work, we are building in Miraflores a community health center, spacious and comfortable for them to work in." ...

The building that they constructed was nicer than a lot of the hospitals that we have seen in other rural areas. It was spacious, but it was also bare. We were grateful because it had possibilities, and it was easier to have crowd control. People brought tables and chairs from their homes so that we could have places to put our equipment and medicines and to be able to sit and talk to patients. They also made makeshift cots to be used as examination and surgery tables.

* * * *

After having to cancel our medical caravan to Sucre twice during the past year (due to the guerrilla activity in the area), we were able to finally return in March of 1996. Our team consisted of one national dentist, two national doctors, one health promoter, Jeni, Jim and Marilyn Oliver (missionaries), and Robert and me. It is a seven-hour trip in four-wheel drive vehicles, and then another eight hours by dugout canoe. You can see God's spectacular handiwork in all its beauty and wonder on this trip: cruising down a tropical river and stream in a dugout canoe; being serenaded by a million, humming mosquitos; watching breath-taking colorful macaws, parrots and other tropical birds flying above us; seeing monkeys swinging in the trees; hearing and seeing howler monkeys roaring like lions, sounding like they were miles away, but actually were above our heads; huge iguanas sunning themselves on the branches; and sloths slowly climbing the tree trunks. We left Barranquilla at 4:00 AM and arrived at the church in Sucre at 9:00 PM. The local people there go out of their way to make our stay as comfortable as possible. Our workday started at 8:00 AM we worked until 12:00 or 12:30, stopping for lunch and a rest beginning the afternoon work at 2:00 PM finishing at 7:00 PM. One night, we finished our surgery at 8:00 PM. It is interesting doing surgery with chickens, dogs, and pigs running under the operating table. We spent one week attending seven hundren medical consults, doing seventy-four pap smears, twenty-nine school physicals, sixty surgeries, and attending sixty dental patients. We were able to work in the new *puesto de salud** that the people had just finished constructing the week before. They had reason to be proud of their work and hopefully it will provide a service and a blessing to the people in the area. It has cement block walls with a cement floor, and fiberglass roof. The mayor of Majagual visited us to thank us for our work in the area, and we thanked him for the economic help of the local government in the construction of the building. This mayor was voted the best mayor in Colombia, and the people in the area said that he truly deserved the honor. (He was kidnapped a couple of months later but released after several months captivity)

The organization of the community in helping the medical caravan was very impressive. Under the leadership of the local pastor, Tulio, committees were formed and everyone worked and participated. Small girls swept the rooms where we slept; others scooped up the animal droppings in the yard and swept the dirt to keep the area clean. Others washed clothes and surgical drapes in the creek, (we later sterilized the drapes to reuse in surgery). Some cooked our meals. A group of young boys formed a water brigade and brought water in plastic jugs collected from a well about a block away (the local well was not working at the moment, but the mayor promised to send money to repair it). There were people constantly providing us with *agua de coco** to drink all day long. The temperature for several days was 105°F. They provided Robert with his *tinto**. There were groups that carried out the surgical patients in hammocks after the surgery and hung the hammocks under the trees until the patient recovered from the anesthesia. Anything that we needed, someone was available to help us. There were people assigned to control the crowds, and others that passed out tracts and witnessed. There were people in charge of the evangelistic services at night. There was a group in constant prayer for the caravan. An older couple was to be married on Sunday after church services. Their children and grandchildren were all ready to participate. With all the red tape and cost of legally getting married, many people in the country do not, or cannot get married. They have what they call "free union" or as we call it common law marriages.

After the church service, the pastor's wife called me over and asked if I could help two of the young men who were to play the guitars and provide the music. They were standing apart with a group of people, and the two young men had ties hanging around their necks; no one knew how to tie them. They asked if I would tie their ties. Everyone was staring because none of them had ever worn a tie before. Even the groom did not have a tie. Tying the ties of the young men was a big social event with a lot of laughter and admiration from the crowd. The wedding party started from the couple's house, which was very close to the church. The musicians led the parade, and everyone else fell in line with the bride and groom close to the front. Everyone sang and clapped all the way to the church. The music was mostly original, written especially for the couple, with a guitar and tambourine accompaniment. The words and rhythm reminded me of Cajun music.

That afternoon, Jim Oliver, baptized eleven people, including the newlyweds, in the creek in front of the church. Robert and I took turns between surgeries to watch the baptisms.

Pastor Tulio came to Barranquilla the following week to pick up the furniture and equipment that Pro Salud and the clinic were donating to the *puesto de salud**. He said that the military arrived in the area the night before we left. They arrived in Miraflores the day that we left. Several guerillas were killed, but none of the church people were hurt. The power of prayer at work! The testimony of this small group of believers has had a big impact in the area.

* * * *

As the guerrillas became more in control of the different areas where we worked, we were unable to return. The people living there are periodically visited and threatened by the guerrillas, vigilantes, paramilitary groups, and military—none of whom wear white hats. The guerrillas come and demand food, money and shelter, and will even conscript the young people. If the people resist, they are killed. The next group comes and punishes the people for "collaborating with the enemy" and sometimes they will line the "collaborators" up and shoot them. The people are caught in the middle of a rock and a hard place.

* * * *

An excerpt from our Christmas Newsletter 1996: ... This has been a good year in some ways and very frustrating in others. The violence has escalated, and we have been advised not to travel outside of the big cities. This also means that Robert has not been able to go bird-watching which, as many of you know, is his big hobby, his way of relaxing and getting rid of tension.

The unemployment level has reached an all-time high, and so many of our people are suffering from extreme poverty. One family in our church, who in the past has reached deep into their own pocket to help someone in need, found themselves in great need. They are a family of six adults living at home, with none of them having a job at the moment. We found out by accident that they had gone two days without food in the house, and they never complained. They remained faithful, working in the missions (without pay), and they never said anything or asked for help. They said that they knew that the Lord would take care of their needs. The church was able to show their love and gratefulness for the many years of faithfulness of this family by taking up a love offering and also giving them the food basket that we collect for those in need.

The city has begun digging to install pipes for water and sewage for the barrio of Villa San Carlos. No telling how long it will take to install and start functioning. The people have only been waiting 6 years for these services. I have been discipling three ladies—Mabel, Luz Marina, and Nuris—who each have five or six children ages three to fourteen. They were talking about schooling their children. They could only send two or three of them to school because they didn't have money for the entrance fee ($20.00). In addition to the entrance fee and the transportation, they have to buy uniforms, books and supplies. We were able to find help for their children, but there are so many more in the same condition. These are public schools and are not supposed to charge fees, but when the government doesn't pay the salaries or expenses of the schools for six months or more, they have to have some income to continue to function. We don't realize in the States how fortunate that we are. We have public schools, private schools or home-schooling. These mothers only have the option of public school. They can barely read themselves and want a better life for their children.

Robert has been chief of surgery and also chief of the emergency room all of this year. Officially, he is only on call every three months for ten days at a time, but in reality, there are few nights that he is not called out for consults or emergency surgery.

* * * *

In November 1997, we returned to Miraflores with a team consisting of one Colombian Doctor, a health promoter, Jeni, John Long, (a volunteer cardiovascular surgeon from the States), and Robert and me. We did 56 surgeries in four and a half days and saw somewhere close to 400 general medical patients. John was a real trouper. When he was not helping Robert with surgery, he attended many general medical consults, something he had not done since his internship. He worked along side us, <u>sweated</u> with us, and pitched in wherever he was needed. We did not finish surgery until seven or eight each night. The pueblo now has a generator so we had lights at night. When the sun went down, the mosquitos came out. There were clouds of them that came out to feed, covering the patient as well as the surgery personnel. I had to spray insecticide to try to keep the population down. One night, while the two surgeons were operating, they yelled at me to "get the bat." I thought that they were teasing about all the mosquitos, but in reality, the spray had disoriented a bat, and he had landed on the back of John's gloved hand. He casually threw the bat off to the floor, and they continued the surgery while I chased the bat. Fortunately, the bat did not land in the wound. Never a dull moment!

The guerrillas were in control of most of that remote area. We knew that we had treated some in the course of our stay, but when some known *moscas** began asking questions about when we were leaving, the pastor and the group that had been praying for the team decided that we needed to leave early. Our people spread the word that we would leave on Thursday morning at 5:00 AM, but we silently slipped out on Wednesday morning at 3:00 AM. When the guerillas arrived early Thursday looking for us, they were told that Dr. Edwards had received an emergency message and had to return to the clinic.

The local pastor of that pueblo called us to make sure that we had returned home without any problems. He expressed his deep gratitude for the team who was willing to go to the "boondocks" where there was no running water or electricity, where the temperature reached 105° F, where we worked hard without complaining, where we shared God's love and blessings with the people there. They did not have money to go to the nearest doctor or drugstore that was a six-hour dugout canoe ride away.

We were never able to return to that area. It was dangerous for us to work there as well as dangerous for the people to whom we minister.

*   *   *   *

An excerpt from letter to a friend in 1998:..... .Thank you so much for your interest and compassion for our Colombian brethren. Your gifts would be greatly appreciated, but we would appreciate if whatever is done is done without publicity. We just received an eighteen-page security briefing and we are urged to keep a low profile. Any time that our names appear in the news, we are inundated with request for help. We already receive close to one hundred request a day that we are unable to help. We have to be very discerning and prayerful about those we are able to help. We just got back from doing medical clinics in a displaced persons camp (internal refugees) where we saw more than five hundred patients in just two days. The needs there are overwhelming, and we can do only so much.

It is not only the bombardment of request for help, but the very real danger of getting our name on the top-wanted list for a long, unwanted vacation with the "unfriendlies."(Leftist guerillas) This practice has increased during this season, and they are looking for new blood. The daughter of a good friend of ours was just released after almost nine months captivity. Any American help at the moment has to be downplayed or not mentioned. I know that this all sounds dramatic and you did not feel the tension when you were here, but the people surrounding you looked out for you as did the Lord. We feel His presence and His love and do not live in constant fear, but we also do not want to tempt Him when He sends us warnings through other people and groups and circumstances.

※ ※ ※ ※

Of the twenty-six years working in Colombia, the year 1998 was one of the most difficult. The increased violence, insecurity, rise of common crimes, the murder of a good friend and colleague, the inability to travel by land outside our large cities caused a lot of tension, frustrations, and cabin fever. We had to cancel all of our mobile medical caravans because the guerrillas control the areas.

Some have asked, "If it is so bad, why don't you leave?" In spite of the escalating violence, we have seen an explosive response to the Gospel. In the last three years, we have seen more than forty new missions or new works open up just in Barranquilla. This is more than in the twenty preceding years all together. It is nothing that we have done, but we are excited to be allowed to be a part of it. Our big concern at the present is training leaders for each of these works. We are planning different levels of training: one for those who do not read well, and one for those who are well-educated. One in our group is preparing a guide for those who cannot read, and Robert is doing all the drawings and illustrations.

Mabel is a new Christian who has gone through a lot of difficult times: she has four children; her husband has difficulty finding gainful employment; her father has had several strokes; her oldest son was diagnosed with heart valve problems. She herself came down with TB for the second time in thirteen years, and we thought that we would lose her. However, she has responded to treatment, and now her lungs are clear. Their landlord forced them to move out of their home. They didn't have enough money to send all their children to school. Thanks to a U.S. Sunday school's financial aid, they are now able to send all their children to school. We were able to help them buy cement so that they could build their own two-room dwelling. Mabel's response to all of this was, "Isn't God good!"

Take all of the problems mentioned above—the blessings, the witnessing, and the explosive response—and multiply them by hundreds, and you will have a glimpse of what is happening here.

Robert and I have begun discipling a young couple, Nicolás and Marta. Last year, I began discipling Marta, but she was always busy or not at home when I arrived. During the study she acted like she did not have any idea what was going on. I felt that she was not ready, and we suspended the studies. This year, Marta approached me, saying that she and her husband had made professions of faith and wanted to be discipled. Robert and I began going to their home on Sunday evenings after choir practice. Robert and Nicolás sat on rocks outside the house, and Marta and I sat inside on boards placed across old chair frames. Neither one reads very well, but they read, reread and reread until they understand what the verse says. Sometimes it takes three to four sessions to get through one lesson. Never-the-less they are learning and understanding, and it is a joy to see their faces light up when they finally have read and understood the passage.

We are unable to travel outside the city, but the opportunities are opening up in the city everywhere. At least, we can sleep in our own beds at night. Even though these areas are in the city, some of them are in such bad conditions that you need four-wheel-drive vehicles to get into them. The area where Mabel, Marta and Nicolás live is on a small hill with no paved roads; they finally got running water from the city (it comes in two times a week), they have electricity of sorts, but no sewage. The sewage runs down the middle of the street. When it rains, which it does often and abundantly, the streets become smelly mud bogs and sometimes the water stands a foot or more deep. The main road (the only entrance into the area) is so eroded that it keeps collapsing. We usually have to park the car and walk about fifteen to twenty blocks up and down over rocky, uneven, sewage filled pathways.

*   *   *   *

In the spring, I received a call from a Kogi mother asking if she and her baby could stay with us while the local doctor was treating the baby. She, the baby, the grandmother, plus two other children showed up at my door. Elizabeth and Orman Gwynn (retired missionaries from Brazil and at present consultants with the IMB) were staying with us at the time, so we only had one available bedroom. We ran out of beds, so we made pallets on the floor and hung hammocks. The interesting part was the story that the grandmother told us. She asked if I remembered going to her village and visiting in a home where a young mother had given birth to a baby boy four hours earlier. How could I forget, as that was where I ate the famous rat soup! She was that mother, and the baby boy was now seventeen years old. She and three of her children were now Christians. As Mabel said, "Isn't God good!".... .

*   *   *   *

One of our missions in Los Cedros is planning an evangelistic campaign in an urbanization next to the mission. We have formed a choir from the mission church to sing special music at the services. Our local church is also preparing a Christmas musical/cantata/drama with the combined adult and children's choir. There is a group of young deaf men signing as the choir sings.

Chapter 6

Para no Consarle con el Cuento

(To make a long story short)

The Colombian Baptist National Convention was scheduled to be held in Cali January 1999. We had made arrangement to attend and then leave from Cali to vacation in Ecuador. The Cali cartel was very active at that time, and we were told by our Colombian brethren and colleagues that it was not safe for us to go to Cali. Since we had canceled all of our activities for two weeks, we decided to spend the whole time in Ecuador. We e-mailed our friends Lois and Delbert Taylor and asked them to make reservations for us at the guest house in Quito. They invited us to stay with them and Delbert offered to be our chauffeur. Robert is an expert bird-watcher and had picked out several areas that he wanted to look for specific birds. We went to a cloud forrest area called Bella Vista where we stayed in a three-story geodesic dome which was built on the edge of a cliff. In the center of the building was a circular ladder with what I called a fireman's pole in the center. We held on to it in order to climb to our third floor room where we slept on mats on the floor. We did have hot showers, and we also had a private balcony. The cost for the three of us was $35 dollars a night, and this included three meals a day. The owner was a personable Englishman. The dietician was a vegetarian from Germany. We were leery at first to find this out but her meals were interesting and very delicious. The birding guide was from Mississippi. There were balconies all around the dome on each level with many bird feeders. I sat on the balcony most of the day and saw all the birds that I could ever want to see while Robert and Delbert tromped through the cloud forrest in the rain, mud, and cold and saw maybe half the birds that I did.

The next day, we drove on to Mindo and stayed at a *pensión** (boarding house) which cost us $1.50 a night with no meals. The first night, as we were getting into bed, it broke and went crashing to the floor. The owners, who were outside our door, heard and were very embarrassed. They came in, and with many apologies, they helped remove the bed frame and place the mattress on the floor. After spending the night before on a thin mat on the floor, this was no problem for us. We laughed it off.

We arose at 3:30 the next morning to go to a "hotel" that had horses and a guide to take us up to the Cock of the Rock Lek (a mating display area for the Cock of the Rock birds). The guide asked who was the better rider. Delbert, having grown up in Oklahoma and spending time breaking horses, got the better horse. Robert got the next best, and I got the swayback old nag that did not want to go up the mountain. Delbert rode in front of me, pulling my horse up the steep, narrow mountain trail. It was pitch black, with no moon, but the guide had a flashlight with batteries that must have been a year old. The beam penetrated the dark up to the horses' ears—his horse. We had been told that the trip would take only forty-five minutes and after only one and a half hours, we arrived at the top. We tethered the horses and then we had to slip and slide down the muddy embankment to reach the area to await the crossing of the Cock of the Rock. I had seen pictures, and they were spectacular birds. We actually saw several fly overhead, and they were almost worth waiting for. We then had to climb back up the embankment to reach the horses. Delbert was in front of me pulling while Robert was behind pushing, and they finally got me up. Unfortunately, I had to get back on that nag and go down the mountain. By then, the wind was blowing, and it was raining. I enjoy horses when I am standing on the ground looking up at them, but I am not a good rider. I pleaded with the Lord that if He got me down off that mountain safe and sound without making a fool of myself, I promised that I would never get on another horse. I have kept that promise. When we reached the "hotel", I could not dismount. It took four of the men to pull me off the horse, and as I stood on the beautiful ground all doubled over, frozen, and unable to straighten up, those four fellows were doubled over laughing. It wasn't funny—then. When we arrived back at our *pensión*, the owner's wife took one look at me and felt pity. She boiled two, big pots of water for my bath. There was one bathroom for all the rooms. The shower consisted of a pipe coming out the wall with cold running water—when there was water. The hot "bath" felt good. While we had been going up the mountain, the owners had brought in a new bed for us. After my hot bath, I climbed in under the covers and slept for a while. The fellows went walking back up the mountain and saw several of the Cock of the Rock without going up as far as we had gone that morning. When they got back to the room, the bath water was cold, and the lady did not offer to heat it up for them. It was Wednesday, and Delbert, Robert and I planned to go to church that night. Robert looked for a change of clothes after his bath. He had worn the same blue jeans for three days, and they were rank from tromping through brush, rain, and mud. Unfortunately, he had left his clothes in Quito at Delbert's house, so had nothing clean to change into. There was no way that he could wear those jeans to church. Desperate, he tried on a pair of my khaki slacks. They were a little short, the zipper would not close completely, and the waist was open, but it had belt loops and he did have a belt. He wore a long-tailed shirt untucked, and since it was cold, he wore a long jacket. Away we went. When we got to the little country church, the pastor asked Robert to preach. There was no pulpit for Robert to hide behind, so he sort of scrunched down and began to preach. Delbert and I were rolling in the pew laughing. Delbert said, "What would the people back home think if they knew that their Baptist Missionary was preaching in a Baptist church in Ecuador wearing his wife's slacks?"

We had such a wonderful time relaxing and being silly. We had not realized how stressed out we were.

* * * *

In 1999, the International Mission Board started what was called New Directions. We divided into teams and were targeting people groups. We were part of the Colombia North Coast Team.

Excerpts from the profile of the Colombia North Coast Team: ... The North Coast of Colombia, South America, is an area currently responsive (explosively responsive) to the Good News of Jesus Christ. Although 90 to 95% of the population is nominally Catholic, most have never heard what it means to have a personal relationship with Jesus Christ or to have the assurance of eternal life. Facing unprecedented violence from civil warfare, drug trafficking, and common crime in the midst of a critical economic situation, Colombians in the area are looking for hope. As a result, many new church starts have recently sprung up.

The major cities of the coast include Barranquilla, Cartagena, and Santa Marta. These cities are the destinations of many refugees fleeing violence. The North Coast Team is targeting the people of the lower and lower middle social classes, a population in which many basic human needs go unmet. Thirty-one percent of the population is fourteen years of age or less. Spanish is the language of the majority population, but the semi-desert Guajira peninsula of the coast is the home of the *Wayu** people, who have their own language and culture. The climate of the coast is hot year round, with only two seasons—the rainy season and the breezy season. Often, we are grateful for our God who is our shade from the heat (Isaiah 25:4). Our desire is for everyone on the coast to be able to know this same defense and refuge.

* * * *

An excerpt from letter to Louise McFerren September 1999: ... I have started a class with fifteen young people, ages thirteen to seventeen, in Villa San Carlos. We are using Josh McDowell's book *Truth Works-Making Right Choices*. These kids are so excited about each class and openly participate talking about the difficult choices they have to face each day. They are understanding why they make certain decisions and the results of their decisions, right or wrong. I was so concerned seeing these kids going through rebellious times at home and in the community. Some had come to know the Lord but were being pressured by their peer groups and family circumstances. They are struggling to know God's path and to do the things that would please Him. They discuss their decisions, good and bad, and why they made that decision. They discuss the results and what could have been the result if they had made another decision. They are tempted by drugs, alcohol, stealing, being members of street gangs, and many other things. One young man told his friends that he would not go to shoot pool with them. They got angry and called him all kinds of names and said that they would never speak to him again. He felt terrible and thought that he had lost all his friends. He didn't have the money to go and would have had to steal the money, as his friends did, to play. Also, he would have had to lie to his parents. The immediate results were that he felt terrible and rejected. A couple of days later his friends were speaking to him again, and in fact, showed more respect to him for standing up to them. There had been a fight at the pool hall and a couple of people were wounded from gun shots. Several of the boys were in jail. These kids are the future of Colombia, and we need to show them God's path and pray that they can make a difference to the future of their country.

We are excited about how the people have caught fire about spreading the Gospel. One church has been without a pastor for more than a year, and the people have taken on the responsibility of sharing God's Word. Yesterday, Robert and I were traveling to a *barrio* about thirty minutes from our home to hold discipleship classes, when just before we turned off the main street onto a dirt road, it started raining so hard we could hardly see. The dirt road was about ten inches under water and we had to put the jeep into four-wheel drive to slip and slide down the street. Several yards into the street we picked up two of the church members who had their shoes in their hands and their Bibles in plastic bags under their arms. They were soaking wet from head to toe but were wading back into the barrio to share the Gospel with the new Christians there.

* * * *

An excerpt from letter to Mike and Dunia November 1999: ... The shocks and the whole suspension system in the car (a '83 Toyota land cruiser) went out Sunday. We were checking out the two *barrios* where we planned to work with Global Mission Fellowship (GMF). The *barrios* are forty-five minutes from our house on the worse roads you can imagine. We did not have time to get the problem repaired before the group arrived so we had to limit the weight in the car. I still carried four people plus all the equipment, bottled water and ice, plastic plates and glasses, coffee, etc. I was the organizer and gofer as well as one of the translators. Dad did the same with another group. We had someone in the *barrio* cook the meals. Our car won the prize for being the dirtiest. We had to travel a long stretch of unpaved road that had huge craters full of mud and water. One day it splashed completely over the car and I couldn't see out the front or the back. We had to clean the windshield and back windows as well as the headlights before we left. We were so excited. The Mother Church only has about forty-six members and seventeen of them worked every day, doing door to door evangelization along with the four people from GMF. There were close to two hundred fifty professions of faith in the two *barrios*. We are now busy doing follow up and discipleship with these.

* * * *

An excerpt from Christmas letter 1999: ... Colombia is pictured as people of drugs and violence. It is true that many are involved, but there are so many

Colombians who are God-loving and God-fearing people, and they never get the publicity.

On the North Coast, there are more than 1,000,000 displaced people (internal refugees). This puts a strain on the cities that are being inundated with these refugees who are fleeing the violence where they lived in the country. These refugees mainly consist of women and children, with a few old people. The men and boys are scarce because they have been killed, and those who remain come and form squatters' camps. (Pirated electricity, no water, no sewage, no work, no schooling, no medical care but they are alive, and many depend on begging, robbing, and prostitution to exist). We are working with many of these groups. In addition to health clinics, we have classes led by Jeni Hester and her ProSalud group who are teaching women to make children's clothing and underwear to sell. They are placing sewing machines in strategic places so that the women can sign up to use and make items to sell. This will help them have a small income. Out of their first sale, we have them put aside a small amount in savings, and also pay a small fee for the upkeep of the sewing machines. This way they are helping themselves and also have pride in taking care of the machines. Unfortunately, many of these camps are built in low lying areas prone to flooding. This year, we have had excessive rain fall, and these areas are all under water. Since these people don't have anywhere else to go, they hang their hammocks a little higher and continue living in their flooded dwellings, sometimes in knee-deep water. Needless to say, these people are suffering from constant skin irritations, gastrointestinal diseases, malnutrition and many stress related problems.

Refugee dwelling made of plastic bags, scraps of wood and tin.

* * * *

I ask several people who have traveled with us on medical caravans to give their personal opinions of this work. One of the most interesting responses came from Jorge G., a young pastor who went with us on a couple of caravans. He made these comments:

"The things that impressed me were the extreme heat and living conditions of the people; the extreme tiredness of our team; and the quantity of heavy, fatty food that we ate. The long, hot, uncomfortable, exhausting trip to arrive at our destination. As there was no electricity, I had to hold the flashlight for the surgeries. I thought that I would pass out. It impressed me how the people traveled under difficult conditions and for long distances to receive treatment. The cooperation of the people was wonderful. They provided for all our needs, swept, washed our clothes in the creek, prepared our food and provided us with coconut water or fruit juice all day long. They waited in long lines to pay their fifty cents or dollar fee that included being seen by the doctor, medicine if it was needed, and surgery if indicated. If they could not pay this amount, they paid with an egg, a turtle, a chicken, coconut, or volunteered to help out. No one was turned away because they could not pay, but everyone wanted to cooperate in some way. I made the mistake of going into the kitchen area while the women were preparing the meal. Chickens were on top of the table pecking away at food with their beaks and squirting it out at the other end. Flies were covering the area. Chickens, turkeys, dogs and pigs were running around and under the table. I lost my appetite. The outhouse contained a ceramic bowl without a toilet seat, and you flushed the contents by pouring creek water, held in a bricked-off corner, down the bowl to flow out into the yard area outside the outhouse. The parking lot, during the rainy season, was dugout canoes lined up on the creek bank; during the dry season, was horses lined up at the fence. There are no proper roads, and the people only have transport by canoe, horseback or walking. The ingenuity of the people was impressive. The post-op patients were carried to the recovery room in hammocks that were tied to a large bamboo pole. The recovery room consisted of hammocks hung under the trees. When the patient recovered enough, he/she either walked home or was carried in the hammock. They sometimes had to walk two hours or two days to get home. During the rainy season, they put the patient in the bottom of the canoe and poled home."

Women preparing our meal in a rural kitchen, notice the pig, dogs, ducks, and chickens

Post-surgery patient being carried home in rural ambulance—hammock tied to bamboo pole

* * * *

An excerpt from e-mail to our daughter-in-law April 1999 … Zully is an eighteen-year-old unwed mother and the sister of Daniel, the street gang member that I mentioned before. I began discipleship classes with her last week. I wish that you could have seen her face and reaction. The father had abandoned the home. No one in the family has a job. She has difficulty getting along with her mother. However, Zully said that she has never felt as loved and at peace as she does now. She could hardly wait to share with a cousin what she had learned.

Isabel, a new believer who was baptized on Easter Sunday, has become Zully's spiritual mentor. Isabel has seven children, and her husband has recently lost his job. Five of the children are school age, but they can only afford to send one to school. Last week, she came to me saying that they had had nothing to eat for three days, only black coffee. The ladies in one of the Bible studies gathered together a cup of rice, a few beans, and a quart of milk and presented a small food basket to Isabel. These ladies have nothing either, but felt that next time, it might be one of them in need.

It is amazing how many people here can't read or write. Well, maybe not so amazing when you look at the cost of public schools and people like Isabel and Mabel who have to choose which child will get an education. We have developed discipleship materials in picture form, and I am using this to disciple three people in Villa San Carlos and four ladies in Villa María. They are excited that they can "read" the discipleship materials. It is exciting to me to watch them as they learn about God and His Love and Salvation.

There are many more individuals who have been affected by the Gospel. Missions are all about people, not in-group form, but as individuals. To see the changed lives, to see their excitement, and to encourage them in their pilgrimage with the Lord is worth all the inconveniences of living under these conditions.

Last night, the house behind our building, along our back drive, was trashed. The doors were torn off, the lavatories torn out of the wall, all the light fixtures ripped out and the house generally destroyed. The people who had lived there had suddenly left the day before. We discovered that they were relatives of a mayor in one of the cities in Sucre, and the guerrillas had a contract out on them. When the family learned of this, they fled for their lives. We did not hear anything. Of course, it is always noisy here. There is a night watchman who walks the streets at night blowing his whistle continually until we all want to shove it down his throat. All it does is clue the bad guys that he is coming, and they hide until he passes. Where was he while this was going on?

* * * *

Debs Cofer and his wife, Marsha are dear friends from Lake Jackson, Texas. Our missionary team was looking for someone in the States to be our prayer co-coordinator, someone to send our e-mail and snail mail prayer letters and request out to all our prayer partners. Deb's name kept coming to my mind. I sent him an e-mail asking him if he would be interested in doing this for us.

Debs replied that he had felt God wanted him to do something in missions. Wednesday night, at church, he had prayed asking God for directions. When he returned home, he opened my e-mail. Debs came to Colombia and spent a week following us around to see the work in order to better assist us in communication efforts.

* * * *

An excerpt from e-mail to Debs Cofer on 3 June 1999 ... Have you heard about the guerrillas kidnapping more than one hundred people including men, women and children, who were attending Mass at a Catholic church in Cali this past Sunday? The daughter of one of Robert's colleagues was among those kidnapped. She has two children. The Catholic Church is so incensed that it has excommunicated the guerrillas. They (the guerrillas) couldn't care less.

Last night, at the Bible Study in Villa San Carlos, we had a little excitement. There were about thirty adults and sixty children and as I was leading the study, a woman ran up and told Victoria (the lady with the crutch) that there was a group of men attacking some people between the highway and us. The police were already there. Everyone jumped up, closed and locked the windows and doors, and told me to continue, so I did. Fortunately, there was no gunfire and things ended quietly. This is a typical event nowadays.

Pray for the people of Colombia. They live under tremendous pressures every day. Either their immediate family, extended family, or friends have either been killed, kidnapped, or they themselves are under threats. The Lord is working in spite of this, or maybe because of it. The people are responsive and hungry to find peace and refuge in the Lord.

* * * *

Excerpts from a letter written by Dr. Sandra Gustin in 1999 ... "God's name is not mentioned in the book of Esther, but the point is obvious. God worked in the life of Esther, preparing her to be in the right place at the right time and meeting a life-and-death need of her people in order to bring honor to God (Esther 4:14, 8:16) Had Esther not been obedient and risen to the occasion, the personal consequences would have been disastrous. What will be the consequences if God has prepared us to bring honor to His name during the current crisis in Colombia, and we do not rise to the occasion? Consider the following facts:

1. Colombia's economic and social situation is critical. Long-standing violence due to civil warfare, drug trafficking and common crime has reached such an unprecedented level that virtually every Colombian family has been directly touched by violence. Colombia leads the world

in homicides (the number one cause of death in the country) and in kidnapping. There are more than 30,000 killings a year, and approximately 1.2 million internal refugees have been forced by violence and fear to leave their land and their livelihood in order to move to major cities where they live in subhuman conditions. Typically, a family of eight may live in a makeshift shelter on a lot of 3 X 8 meters. Ironically, in the cities, they do not find security or freedom from fear. Skilled in agriculture, they are unprepared for earning a livelihood in the cities, and most do not make even the minimum wage of $80 a month. Due to inflation, the purchasing power is less than it was in 1993 and will be even less in 1999. Two and a half million children are currently forced to work. Severe malnutrition is increasing. Women make up a disproportionate number of refugees due to the deaths of husbands and older sons. Adult illiteracy, always a problem for Colombia, is increasing, as schooling is disrupted or unaffordable, and may be thirty percent or more among the female refugee population. Although electricity is quickly pirated by illegal connections to their new homes, clean water and sewage disposal are not available. Diarrhea and respiratory infections take heavy tolls on the children (thirty-one percent of the Colombian population is fourteen years of age and under; this percentage is higher among refugees). Simple prenatal care is not received. With the devaluation of the peso and the new sales taxes (sixteen percent), costs of medications and staples have skyrocketed. Fifty-five percent of the Colombian population is without health insurance, and those who do have health insurance often find that the money is just not there for them to receive needed care.

2. The Colombia mission is blessed with the presence of medical field personnel (three salaried career missionaries) with long and wide experience in medical evangelism, including working in areas where there is no other evangelical witness. The Voluntariado Integral Comunitario (VIC) (Holistic Community Volunteers) (formerly called ProSalud,) founded and directed by missionary Jeni Hester, is legally recognized in Colombia and has national personnel and infrastructure in place to impact all of Colombia. Trained health promoters (1500 have been trained by VIC; 800 are currently active) can work in places where IMB personnel cannot.

3. Although, using Jesus' own example, meeting human needs is important in and of itself, meeting human needs in Colombia has also been an

effective way to evangelize. In their pain and suffering, Colombians are searching for hope now more than ever. Meeting human needs opens the door to evangelism, and the continuing presence made possible by the structure of VIC lends itself to discipleship and leadership training.

This is a critical moment in Colombia's history. God has prepared us and placed us in position to respond. We ask for your prayers as we face this time ..."

* * * *

During the first three months of 2000, four different Baptist pastors/churches received threats and/or demands for money. While each incident was somewhat different and no threats were carried out, it was very disturbing that these men and their families had been under surveillance for weeks at a time. Pastors from other evangelical groups had also been contacted and threatened in the Barranquilla area—a total of fourteen people were affected. In our home all the pastors, their wives, and all the missionaries met with a team from the *Gaula** (an anti-kidnapping/SWAT team) to discuss how we should all proceed and protect our families and our ministries. They gave us good advice about being alert to our surroundings, to vary our schedules, never travel the same way, not to be predictable, to always check with their offices if we needed to travel (to see if any chatter or violent activity was occurring where we were planning to go), and to report anything unusual that we noticed. Then one of the young *Gaula* officers turned to Robert and said, "Dr. Edwards, you don't know me, but I know you. You operated on my mother. You have treated so many people here on the coast that you are well known. If you changed your modus operandi, it would be very visible. The guerrillas know who you are and your schedule." That didn't exactly reassure us. We were impressed how the pastors responded. They wanted to know how they could protect us. Through the trials and tension, we all formed a close bond to one another.

* * * *

In March 2000, we returned to the States for the wedding of our son, Charles and Lori. The night of the wedding, as Robert was dressing in his rented Tux, he discovered that the cummerbund and the bow tie were missing. Lori was upset, thinking her wedding was ruined. Our family came to the rescue improvising, as we so often had to do in Colombia. We made a bow tie using a piece of left over pew bow ribbon and stapled it to his shirt. We found a piece of black cloth and pleated it and made a cummerbund and stapled it to his pants. No one was the wiser.

* * * *

An excerpt from letter to Volunteer group from Virginia who worked with us for a week in Cartagena in several internal refugee neighborhoods ... I arrived home and found that my computer modem was fried and I will have to send it to the States with someone for Dell to repair. In the meantime, I have to go to a Café Internet to send and receive my e-mail.

I hope each of you recovered quicker than Robert and I. We were beat! As we grow older, it seems to take us longer to recuperate. We are not sick, just worn to a pulp. One of our problems is that we have not had any free time to rest and recoup.

I just wanted to let you know that it was a joy working with each of you. I know that the conditions and the techniques used here were all strange and often opposite to what you are accustomed to or were taught. Under the circumstances, limited equipment, and supplies, and settings, we have found that these techniques work for us, and the Lord blesses our efforts. Each of you has had a great influence on the lives of all those patients and their families. They can see better now with the eyeglasses that you provided, and they will not be overburdened with more children than they can afford to feed and educate. They will have better health instead of constantly being pregnant. They will all have a better standard of living. They appreciate the love and care that you gave them, and many will come to know the Lord because you cared ...

In the sweltering heat and humidity, we did 51 surgeries all using flashlights as our light source. We did a tubal ligation on a twenty-four-year-old woman who had already had five pregnancies—all were twins. Of the ten babies, only three survived. Her health, both physical and mental, was shot. Hopefully, she will have a better lifestyle now. Another girl was twenty-eight years old and already had eight children. These are people who live in the dwellings made of cardboard or plastic with dirt floors and no water or sewage and pirated electricity.

* * * *

His sister, Elena, who lived in the refugee camp with her 5 children, brought Marcos, a forty-year-old farmer, to us. Marcos was in a highly agitated state. He couldn't speak, he couldn't stay still, he walked around in a jerky manner picking things up and putting them down, he stared out of bloodshot eyes looking frantically one way and then another. Elena said that the guerrillas had shown up at the family farm and killed all of Marcos' family before his eyes and then torched his house and lands. They then told Marcos and his farm hand to leave or they would be killed also. Marcos had not spoken since. I started talking to Marcos in a soft, soothing voice and gently, but firmly, put my hand on his shoulder and guided him to a chair. He fixed his eyes on me and seemed to calm down as long as I talked and kept my hand on him. While I sat beside him talking, Robert was able to physically exam Marcos. Physically he was fine, but he was so traumatized mentally that he was unable to function. We were able to help Marcos and Elena get badly needed psychiatric help. The horror of the undeclared war being waged between the guerrillas, the paramilitary, and the military is affecting the whole country. There are so many people like Marcos and Elena who have been traumatized beyond our comprehension. We can only pray for them and try to give comfort in small ways, like seeing that they get medical attention, psychiatric help and spiritual help. There is so much to be done and so little that we can do.

* * * *

We first met twelve-year-old Aliz when she came to one of our mobile medical clinics for treatment. Aliz has a rare, debilitating, congenital skin disease. Her toes and fingers are webbed together and are drying up. The rest of her skin looks like it is rotting off her bones. She is unable to run and play like other children. Fortunately, her beautiful little face is unaffected. She has a sweet personality but becomes depressed at times asking, "Why? Why am I so deformed when my brothers are perfectly formed?" We told her that Jesus created her, as well as her brothers, and that He loved her as she was. In His eyes she was perfect and beautiful, and He had a special purpose for her life. Her eyes lit up, and she wanted to know more about this Jesus. She invited Jesus into her heart. Now, her mother says that she insists that the family read the Bible together every day. When we showed Aliz how to use a liquid bubble solution to blow bubbles, her contagious giggles brought tears to our eyes as she hobbled about trying to pop the bubbles. Her mother cried as she said that she had not heard Aliz giggle like that for years. Aliz's parents have now become Christians and were baptized in the Caribbean Sea. Because of her delicate skin condition, we had to baptize Aliz in clean, fresh water. We brought the water from our house to fill a barrel in front of her home where her family and neighbors were able to witness and share in this joyous occasion.

* * * *

Aldo, Margarita, and Monica were brother and sisters who lived with their aunt in Barranquilla. Their father worked on a farm out in the country and sent them money for their education, but the guerrillas killed him. Margarita was able to continue her medical studies, but the other two had to suspend their education for the time being. We were able to arrange for Margarita to complete her year of mandatory rural medicine service working with our mobile medical clinic program. Later on, we were able to get scholarships for Monica and Aldo to continue their education.

Aldo studied at the Government University in Barranquilla. He got permission from his English professor to invite Robert and me to teach Christmas Carols in English to their class. We taught them several Carols in English and then taught them some in Spanish. The class and the professor were so excited that they asked if we would direct them to perform before the entire university. We arranged for a small sound system and set up in the main entry to the University. The security for entering this university was tighter than any airport security. You had to enter through a locked iron gate where you and all your belongings were searched. This university had a leftist leaning, and every time there was a rebellion or uprising, it began here. There was no glass in the windows, and there were scars on the walls from the many fire bombings and grenades that had been launched at the building. The university president asked if we would perform again. They set us up in the dinning area, which was in reality a large open room with cement tables and benches. The students used it to congregate but did not eat there. The walls were lined with hundreds of pictures of Che Guevera, the hero of the leftist students. Aldo and a few of the Christian students had received permission to use a small portion of the wall to paint three empty crosses on a hill and print John 3:16 underneath. We had permission to not only sing the Christmas Carols but also to preach the true meaning of Christmas. We had a great response from the students. Several of them asked if we would do the same program in their neighborhoods so that their families could hear it.

Aldo was young, but he had a heart for missions. He wanted everyone to come to know his Lord and Savior. He started several missions outside the city and then asked the missionaries to help him organize them into churches.

*　　*　　*　　*

Our local church was having serious economic problems, as were many other churches throughout the country. We were looking for creative ways to bring in money to fund our different ministries. Our people were willing, but so many of them were out of work and unable to give economically; but did give of their time and talents. A group approached me and asked if I would put together a cookbook using the recipes that I had used in my cooking classes. Aida suggested that I include some of my Bible Studies, the plan of salvation, plus spiritual helps. We struggled with the name for the cookbook. Someone suggested we call it "Cocinando con Dolores" (Cooking with Pain). (My name translated in Spanish means pain) We thought that didn't sound appropriate for a cookbook, so we decided on "Cocinando y Meditando con Doña Dolores" (Cooking and Meditating with Mrs. Dolores). Doña is a respectful title used for a married older woman. Several of our professional young people helped to edit the book and others helped to get it printed. I wrote in the forward the following: "This book is prepared especially for the Christian woman who shares love with the poor, who takes meals to the sick and her neighbors. It is also for Christian women who have preached the Gospel with their lives that are full of the love of God. I have tried to present within these pages the Living Christ for those who yet do not know Him.... May God Bless each housewife who uses this book and may the Holy Spirit help her have a joyful family relation and raise up her children to help construct a strong nation." ... We had five hundred copies printed at first and had to have more printed. It was much better received that we had dreamed possible. A couple of women called and said that they had become Christians after reading the book. All I could say was Praise the Lord.

*　　*　　*　　*

Debs Cofer said that I gave him the following:

YOU MIGHT BE A MISSIONARY TO COLOMBIA IF …

1. You've ever taken a shower out of a bucket … and were grateful.
2. Your idea of a romantic evening is an electric light dinner.
3. You celebrate the arrival of the J. C. Penney catalogue.

4. You have caught yourself inching into high-speed traffic in order to cut it off so you could cross the road.
5. You are cold when it is 70° F.
6. Your child's first words in Spanish were "*se fue la luz*"* (The lights went out.)
7. You have learned that the hour given for an event to start is in fact the time you need to roll out of bed.
8. You worry that your cereal might have gone bad if there were no bugs in it. (After all, why didn't the bugs like it?)
9. You have decided that the only possible reason for having those little dotted lines on the road is to mark where to dig the next sewer line ditch.
10. You take the parasite medicine once a quarter—just for the fun of it.
11. You feel complimented when someone calls you "*gordo*"—(fat)
12. You have to unseal envelopes before you can use them the first time.
13. You have a large water barrel sitting in your shower.
14. You really need to hang your sheets out on the line each morning to dry, but have ceased to care.
15. You have electrical appliances mixed in with sick people on your prayer list.
16. You are ministering outside your gifts and folks actually seem to be edified by it.
17. You have finally learned that Meringue doesn't go on lemon pie. (It is music).
18. You use the term "desalination" to describe your bedtime shower.
19. You can sing off key in an attitude of worship.

*   *   *   *

An excerpt from e-mail to Debs Cofer March 2000 ... I have been frustrated lately. We have been without phone service more that we have had service. As you may remember, just doing ordinary chores, takes time and energy. I had to pay the house/property tax on three of our mission homes. It would be easy if you got the bill and went down and paid it, right? Well, you have to go to one special bank, stand in long lines, get a special check for each house, then go to another bank, stand in even longer lines to pay the taxes. Then, you have to take that receipt and register it in another place after standing again in another long line. This takes up most of one day. Now I have three cars that need car emission tags. It has taken me so far three days working on these and I still lack completing the work. Just common chores are time consuming. Enough complaints. The work is really exciting. Last weekend, we went on a mobile medical trip to Cartagena and worked in two different refugee camps. In two and a half days we attended more than six hundred seventy patients. You remember the neighborhood where you were impressed with the spider web electric wires (pirated electricity wires)? Well, these two neighborhoods are even more primitive.

In the mission in Villa San Carlos (where you met my young ex-street gang member), they are excited about planning a three-night evangelistic revival service. They have everything planned down to the follow up of new Christians. There are two couples that have lived together for many years without the benefit of legalizing their unions, and they have asked us to legally wed them. They are all new Christians and now feel the need to be right before God and men. They have asked Robert and me to be *padrinos** at each of these unions.

Pray for José M. who drives a propane gas truck to various villages. The guerrillas have stopped him several times, and the last time was told not to return if he wanted to keep his truck and his life. Pray for him and many like him. This is their livelihood, the only way they can make a living. In the Chocó, where we used to go regularly, the guerrillas attacked and barbarously killed twenty-six military young men and ten civilians this past weekend. We have heard that all of our people are ok but some are in hiding for the moment. We have been unable to go there for about three or four years ...

* * * *

We had a volunteer group from the States that was helping with medical clinics in poor neighborhoods. We had about three tables set up in a small room where doctors and translators were seeing patients. I was translating for one of the American doctors. We all shared another room in the house that gave us a little privacy for examining the patients. Dr. Cliff looked up as a patient was coming toward our table and asked me if we had many homosexuals here. I said that we had some. He nodded to the fellow sitting down and asked what I thought. I looked at him and nodded saying, "I think." Well, Cliff asked me to find out if there was any possibility of him being exposed to HIV. I thought, "Dear Gussy, how do I broach that subject." I turned to the fellow and with a smile; I meant to say, "*Tienes una novia?*" (Do you have a girlfriend?) What came out of my mouth was, "*Tienes un novio?*" (Do you have a boyfriend?) All the other translators stopped and turned to me in surprise. The young man after a startled glance and with a very effeminate hand gesture and high voice replied, "Not at the moment." Well I certainly opened up the discussion.

Chapter 7

Cerrando con Broche de Oro

(Finishing well)

Robert was invited to preach and baptize four people in the Caribbean Sea at the little fishing village were we had begun work some thirty years before. This little church was meeting in the back yard of one of the church members. They had a plastic sheet covering the meeting area to protect them from the sun and rain. There were around forty people present and the pastor, Alejandro, who was the nephew of Emilia, (the woman who brought Robert the "two precious eggs"), apologized for not having more people present. The city was without water and the people would not come because they could not bathe. We were impressed with the growth of the church. They wanted us to see the fruits of the seeds that we had planted so many years before. Several of the leaders stood up and said that they had attended the first bible studies that we had held, several had been children at the time, and they wanted to thank us for our labor. We were very touched. This small church has started three missions. It is a church that is producing churches.

* * * *

For the first twenty years that we worked in Colombia, we had the privilege of traveling and working in all parts of the country. We saw more of Colombia than the average Colombian. In the last ten years, we were restricted to the larger cities because of the violence and unrest in the rural areas. Kidnapping, extortion, and assassination were a constant threat outside the big cities, and even in the large cities, we had to be aware of what was happening around us and avoid certain areas of the city. We felt that the Lord used the people in the area to protect us. When they had wind of a possible protest or unrest, they would advise us not to go to that area. When we did go, they always accompanied us to let everyone know that we were known and accepted by the people.

Robert and I were both brought up in the church. When we completed our medical training, Robert went into private practice for six years. We had four children and were active in our church when the Lord called us into full-time missions service. It was a hard decision to make, but one we do not regret. Living in a foreign culture, we have known times of extreme frustration. We often worked under poor or nonexistent medical facilities. We have seen the great need and have known that what we did was not nearly enough to match what was needed. Then we saw the face of Juan after surgery as he kneeled, praising God for His goodness and mercy. Juan was the man mentioned earlier called "the horned one" who lived the life of a hermit because he had a "horn" growing over his eyebrow. It was a large cyst that we were able to remove and now he lives in his village a changed man.

Then there was Zaida who for twenty years had limited use of her right arm due to severe burns. She had burn contractures that prevented her from doing many things. We were able, after five operations, to release these contractures and do some grafting to enable her to have almost full use of that arm. We even did some physical therapy with her. To straighten and strengthen her arm, we had her carry around a heavy bucket.

* * * *

Luke 7:22 says: ... "Go back and report ... what you have seen and heard: The blind receive sight, the lame walk.... the deaf hear, ... and the good news is preached to the poor ..."

We saw all of this happen through modern-day miracles. The blind were able to see again after receiving used eyeglasses that people had donated. After receiving her glasses, Matilde asked for a Bible. Tears ran down her cheeks, as she was able to read her Bible for the first time in years.

The deaf were able to hear again after some received hearing aids, and others learned sign language and were able to "hear" the good news in their own heart language and culture. After receiving her hearing aid, Anna heard a human voice for the first time when she was 25 years old. Alfie came to know the Lord after "hearing" through sign language. He is now the pastor of an "all deaf" church.

The lame walked again. Many who had walked with crutches for years because of amputations were fitted with prosthesis and were able to walk. After receiving her "new leg", Liliana tentatively put her foot down, then walked a few steps, then danced a jig.

*　　*　　*　　*

There were many, many more, too numerous to mention, but just as dramatic. Yes, Lord, it was worth it! He never promised it would be easy but he did promise to always be with us even to the ends of the earth.

*　　*　　*　　*

Our last year in Colombia was hectic. People knew that we would be leaving in February 2003. In 2002, everyone tried to schedule surgery before we left. We were physically and emotionally put through a wringer with fourteen huge farewell parties. The mayor of Barranquilla gave Robert an official commendation of appreciation. Individually and together we received nine plaques of appreciation. We were both invited to speak at various churches and organizations. Robert was interviewed on T.V. The church where we had directed the choir for so many years surprised us; they had invited all the former choir members to sing in our final Christmas cantata. There were thirty-five former and/or present members that participated. The national mission offering, equivalent to our "Lottie Moon Christmas Offering" was named "The Edwards Missionary Offering". This was such an honor. We were overwhelmed with the outpouring of love and honors that were bestowed upon us. We loved these people and they were showing their love for us. It was difficult to leave, but it was time for us to move on to another phase of our lives. Obedience to God has always been our most important objective. We felt from the beginning that we were in Colombia to work ourselves out of a job. We treated many health needs, shared our faith and our Lord with the people. We encouraged them and trained them to do what we were doing. There are many Colombians now who are leading music, teaching, preaching, evangelizing, and establishing churches, which are reproducing themselves. There are Colombian doctors and nurses who are providing medical care for those in need. We were excited to learn recently that one of our Colombian "grandchildren" has been accepted into medical school. The cycle is continuing. We keep in touch with our adopted family and friends through regular mail, e-mail, and occasional phone calls. We have even had the joy of visits from a few who have traveled to the States.

God led us to a beautiful place to retire. We have become active in a wonderful local church. We have had the opportunity to speak about our mission work in many churches and organizations, not only locally, but also in various states. We have the freedom to travel to visit family and friends. This is a freedom that people in the States do not appreciate. We have been on several volunteer mission trips to various countries. God continues to bless us and we look forward to what He has for us in the future.

APPENDIX

Four decades of conflict have turned Colombia into one of the worlds worst humanitarian hot spots, with millions caught up in the crossfire between leftist rebels, cocaine smugglers and far-right paramilitary militias.

In 2001 our team divided so that we could cover other groups of people. Our group was renamed Hope For Today.

An excerpt from web page of Hope For Today team:.... The **Hope For Today** Team is composed of missionaries and Baptist partners united by the objective of reaching all of the socio-economically-disadvantaged people of the Caribbean coast of Colombia for Christ. We believe that God will establish a New Testament church within walking distance of every person in this population segment. We are on a mission with God as we seek ways to evangelize the lost, disciple the believers, equip the leaders and minister to human needs.

The word "**Hope**" is part of our team name because we saw the bondage and resulting despair of our people's daily living and their struggle to rise above it. We know they will find the only answer in Jesus Christ as he brings "**hope**" to their lives. "**Today**" is part of the name because of our conviction that eternal and abundant life begins "**today**" from the moment a person receives Jesus Christ as his Savior.

* * * *

Excerpt Hope For Today web site: ... "The estimated GNP for 1999 was 3%, which was the worst year for the economy of Colombia in the last 100 years. No one really expects this situation to improve, until and unless the political situation changes radically. Since the country has not been able to deal with the roots of the problems, which in turn continue to produce the violence cycle that has been perpetuated for the last thirty years—no one is very optimistic about the economic growth of the country for the next several years.

The minimum salary, which is set annually by the central government in January, has been at 120 to 100 dollars US for the last ten years. During the same period, the cost of living in Barranquilla increased 18% on the US dollar. On top of this a sales tax was instituted in 1997 that is 16% on the peso. This sales tax was expanded to include many food items in 1998. Utility companies have added an item to their monthly bill called a "contribution" which in effect is a price hike that does not require government approval. The people of the popular class, our target group, make $100 US down to $20 US a month. Family members will many times share one home and pool several salaries in order to try and cover most of their expenses each month. Grandmothers often provide childcare so that mothers can also work. Unemployment among the lower strata of society is double the published rate of 21% for the entire country. These statistics do not deal with the problem of underemployment among our target group.

Fifty percent of the population on the coast lives in areas of the cities or in small towns where an adequate water supply and sewage disposal are luxuries. Most people do have electricity in their homes. Cooking may be done on a kerosene stove, gas range, electric hot plate, or wood fire in the backyard.

If an adult can read and write his name, he is considered to be literate. 90% of our people are oral learners.

Only 16% of the children of the popular class will finish high school, although this percentage is probably higher among evangelicals, and very few will be able to attend college. Vocational training programs are swamped. The government sponsored vocational program, SENA, has not been able to maintain its enrollment for the past three years because of budget cuts. Private vocational programs are becoming more and more expensive.

By law all Colombians have universal health care coverage. But in practice, the government's system is overloaded and under funded due to the internal turmoil of the country. A large percentage of health care needs go unattended. Public health care problems are on the rise." …

* * * *

An excerpt from the website of Hope For Today team: … The population of the country is just more than 40 million. It is projected that the population for year 2010 will be 45.5 million, although birth rates in some areas of the country are dropping …

The majority of the people on the coast (around eight million) live in the department (state) capitals of Barranquilla, Cartagena and Santa Marta. By the end of 1999, almost one out of every two people living in Cartagena was a refugee. The population of the city increased from 700,000 to 1,200,000 in two years. This same phenomenon is happening in Santa Marta, where there is a critical lack of fresh water. Although the region has many small towns which vary in population from 2,000 to 15,000 and are generally agricultural or fishing centers, particularly in the departments of Bolivar and Magdalena, the people are being forced to abandon their small farms or businesses in increasing numbers and are migrating to the urban centers. This "displaced" population is growing rapidly. These people who were self-sufficient, i.e., able to feed themselves, are forming squatter communities on the fringes of the larger towns and cities and are destitute. These are the surviving victims of the on-again, off-again civil war that began in 1948 with the assassination of Galan. The conflict is between the central government troops and left-wing dissidents, which number somewhere between 15,000 and 40,000 members. The left-wing groups are divided into three principal guerilla armies, FARC, ELN, and EPL and several very radical small cells, which operate independently. The situation is complicated by the very lucrative illegal traffic in cocaine and opium and the right-wing paramilitary vigilante groups. The fighting between all these groups has served to create serious social and economic turmoil throughout the country. This is manifested by high and rising unemployment among professionals, skilled laborers, and unskilled laborers, bankrupt socialized medical programs, which means fewer and fewer people have access to any health care, increasing hunger among the poor, closure of schools, both private and public, and lack of housing—people are not able to pay mortgages and are losing their homes. There has been a sharp rise in urban and family violence from the year 2000 to 2002. During the years 1965-1985, the majority of the population ignored guerilla activities, which generally occurred in the countryside. These disturbances were perceived as being very removed from the cities. That has changed gradually, until everyone is being directly affected by the political, economic, and social unrest in the country.

Among the displaced people, the government has found that 80% of the estimated 2,000,000 internal refugees in the country are single (many widowed) women and children. Only 20% are males over the age of eighteen. The population of Colombia continues to be young with 58% of the population being under the age of twenty-four. 36% of the population is under the age of fifteen. This demographic represents the population on the north coast ...

GLOSSARY OF SPANISH WORDS AND PHRASES

- Agua de coco—coconut water
- Agua de panela—popular drink made of raw sugar, water and lemon
- Aguacera—torrential down pour (rain)
- Aguardiente—a type of cheap liquor
- Año rural—(AHN-yo ru-RAL) year of government medicine in a rural area required to obtain your medical license
- Arroyo—dry riverbed
- Arroz con verduras—rice and vegetables
- Barrio—(BAH-ree-o) neighborhood
- Borojó—(bo-row-HOE) fruit that is indescribably horrible, taste like dirty rotten rags
- Cabañas—cabins
- Café con leche—coffee milk
- Campecino—country boy
- Cedula—(SAID-u-lah) identity card
- Chontodura—Palm fruit that is shaped like a large acorn, but orange in color. It is fibrous and the longer you chew it the more fibrous it becomes. It is like chewing on soft wood.
- Contrabandista—dealer in contraband, smuggler

- Corozos—another type of fruit from a palm tree. It has large seeds about the size of a marble. Makes a delicious juice. I used it to replace cranberry juice.
- Dulce quemada—literally means burnt sugar. It is a dark brown liquid sugar. Mixed with granulated white sugar it makes brown sugar.
- Embera—Indian tribe living in the Chocó—area where Colombia borders with Panama.
- Finca—(FINK-ca) farm
- Gaula—Government anti-kidnapping/SWAT team
- Gordo—fat
- Gringa—North American female
- Gringo—North American male
- Hunchaka—(HUN-cha-kah) Kogi Indian greeting meaning hello, how are you.
- Kogi—Indian tribe living in northern Colombia in the Sierra Nevada Mountains.
- La Batalla de Flores—The Battle of the Flowers. Main parade of Carnival
- La Esperanza—(Lah s-pear-RAN-zah) Hope
- Mama—Kogi Indian witch doctor, shaman, spiritual leader.
- Mochila—(mo-CHEE-lah) Woven, over the shoulder rucksack. Kogi Indian men wear two crisscrossed over their chest. It is the custom to exchange coca leaves, (which they carry in one of the mochilas) with men they meet on the trail. The women use one large one draped over their forehead and hanging down their backs to carry their babies.
- Moscas—literally means flies. Word used for guerrilla spies.
- Padrinos—Godparents
- Palacio de Justicia—Supreme Court building
- Palanca—influence, to pull strings, literally means lever
- Pensión—boarding house
- Pila—(PEE-lah) outside cement sink

- Plátano—(PLAIT-tah-no) plantain
- ProSalud (later called Voluntariado Integral Comunitario or VIC)—An organization that promotes and trains workers in primary health care in areas where there are no doctors. The workers are also trained in evangelization.
- Puesto de salud—health care center
- Reja—grille, or iron bars
- Ruana—(ru-AH-nah) type of poncho
- Sancocho de gallina—(san-COACH-o day guy-YEEN-ah) chicken soup
- Se fue la luz—the lights went out
- Socorro—Help
- Ticuna—Indian tribe living on Amazon River in southern Colombia.
- Tienes una novia—Do you have a girl friend?
- Tienes un novio—Do you have a boy friend?
- Tinto—small demitasse of black coffee
- Transito—Department of Public Safety
- Usted es cupable—You are guilty.
- Wayu—Indian tribe in the northern desert area of Colombia.

SPANISH PHRASES

- Paso a Paso se Va Lejos

Literal translation: Step by step you go far
English phrase: The road to Rome begins but with a single step

- A Buena Hambre, No Hay Mal Pan

Literal translation: For great hunger, there is no bad bread
English phrase: If you're hungry, any food will taste good

- Querer es Poder

Literal translation: To want or to love is to be able
English phrase: Where there is a will, there is a way

- A Grandes Males, Grandes Remedios

Literal translation: Great evils, great solutions
English phrase: Great needs require great solutions

- La Necesidad Abre la Puerta de Muchos Logros

Literal translation: Necessity opens the door to many achievements
English phrase: Necessity is the mother of invention

- Para no Cansarle con el Cuento

Literal translation: For not to tire you with the story
English phrase: To make a long story short

- Cerrando con Broche de Oro

Literal translation: Closing with a gold metal
English phrase: Finishing well

MEDICAL TERMS

- Amenorrhea—Absence of menstruation
- Bells Palsy—Temporary partial paralysis of one side of face
- Bilateral partial brachial plexus palsy—Damaged nerves that go to upper extremity. It produces severe pain, weakness, and diminished reflexes
- Brucellosis—Undulant fever. Often associated with biological warfare.
- Pterygium—an inflammatory growth that sometimes goes from the inside corner of the ever covering the cornea. It can cause blindness.
- URI—Upper respiratory infection

MILITARY TERMS

- ELN—leftist guerrilla group
- FARC—another leftist guerrilla group
- Paramilitary—auto defense groups originally designed to protect from guerrillas. A type of vigilante group.

978-0-595-41599-1
0-595-41599-7

Printed in the United States
81785LV00002B/475-633